P9-BYQ-435

AMERICAN HORTICULTURAL SOCIETY
PRACTICAL GUIDES

GARDENING IN SHADE

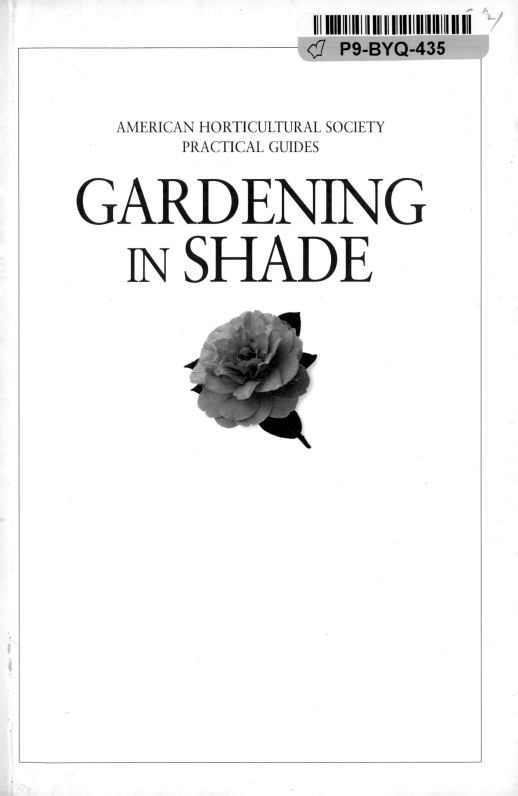

AMERICAN HORTICULTURAL SOCIETY
PRACTICAL GUIDES

GARDENING
IN SHADE

LINDEN HAWTHORNE

DK PUBLISHING, INC.

www.dk.com

A DK PUBLISHING BOOK
www.dk.com

PRODUCED FOR DORLING KINDERSLEY BY PAGEONE,
Cairn House, Elgiva Lane, Chesham, Buckinghamshire

PROJECT EDITOR Charlotte Stock

SERIES EDITOR Pamela Brown
SERIES ART EDITOR Stephen Josland

MANAGING EDITOR Louise Abbott
MANAGING ART EDITOR Lee Griffiths
US EDITOR Ray Rogers

First American Edition, 1999
2 4 6 8 10 9 7 5 3

Published in the United States by
DK Publishing, Inc., 95 Madison Avenue, New York, New York 10016

Copyright © 1999
All rights reserved under International and Pan-American Copyright Conventions.
No part of this publication may be reproduced, stored in a retrieval system, or
transmitted in any form or by any means, electronic, mechanical, photocopying,
recording, or otherwise, without the prior written permission of the copyright owner.
Published in Great Britain by Dorling Kindersley Limited.

Library of Congress Cataloging-in-Publication Data

Gardening in shade. — 1st American ed.
p. cm. — (AHS practical guides)
Includes index.
ISBN 0–7894–4154–3
1. Gardening in the shade. 2. Shade-tolerant plants.
I. DK Publishing, Inc. II. Series.
SB434.7.G27 1999
635.9'543—dc21   98–48214
                                                    CIP

Reproduced by Colourscan, Singapore
Printed and bound by Star Standard Industries, Singapore

CONTENTS

GARDENING IN SHADE 7

The advantages of shade, assessing the shade
in your garden, flowering and foliage plants
that will thrive, and plants for every season

PLANTING PLANS FOR SHADE 25

CARING FOR PLANTS IN SHADE 47

Preparing and planting, routine plant care,
keeping plants healthy and trouble-free

PLANTS FOR SHADE 55

Plants of every type, from trees to spring bulbs,
for light, deep, partial, and dappled shade

GARDENING IN SHADE

ADVANTAGES OF SHADE

IF SHADE DID NOT OCCUR naturally in a garden, it would become necessary to create some – simply because shade is essential to get the best from so many exquisite garden plants. Shade is indispensable in providing interesting planting opportunities and, indeed, it becomes a positive necessity in hot climates.

A WEALTH OF SHADE-LOVERS

Since the range of plants that thrive in shade is immense, gardeners seldom need to feel restricted by the lack of suitable material for growing in shady sites. While there are relatively few shade-loving annuals and grasses, and virtually no water plants, woods and forests have provided a wealth of bulbs, perennials, ferns, and woody plants that can be grown in shady gardens. Such diverse plant types provide unlimited opportunities for the creation of mixed plantings that ensure color and interest throughout the year.

◄WOODLAND NATIVES
Where space is limited, ferns, ivies, and violas can be grown in containers, creating beautiful textural compositions in shady corners. Keep steps and paths clear of moss and algae, which thrive in shade and make conditions dangerous underfoot.

◄COOL SHADE *A cool, shady niche maintains the lush, verdant foliage of ferns and hostas.*

THE BENEFITS OF SHADE

Shady areas in the garden actually increase the range of plants that may be grown successfully. Many natives of forests and woods need shade of some sort; in fact, they are likely to scorch or fail in sunny,

A shady site protects plants against extremes of temperature

open sites. They usually flower better in shade, and their flowers and foliage stay fresh for longer periods.

In a shaded site, it is easy to provide the cool, moist conditions needed by many spring-flowering plants, such as snowdrops, winter aconites, and hellebores, during the summer. Cooler and more humid than an open site, a shady bed is less exposed to

SUN PROTECTION FOR PLANTS
Shade-loving plants such as sweet woodruff (Galium odoratum) *need protection from the hottest sun if they are not to suffer from sun scorch in summer, especially in hotter regions.*

TYPES OF SHADE

- LIGHT shade is cast by buildings, walls, or fences onto sites that are open to the sky.
- DAPPLED shade is cast by the canopy of deciduous trees when in full leaf.
- PARTIAL shade is temporary and moves with the sun's passage through the sky.
- DEEP shade occurs beneath evergreen trees or in sunless alleys between tall buildings.

extremes of temperature in summer and winter and, depending on the type of shade, it may be better able to retain soil moisture. Shade reduces the need for watering, and it ensures that plants look lush and verdant in mid- to late summer, when those in sun may be past their best.

Sunless sites may be cold during the winter months, but their low temperatures help discourage dormant plants from emerging too early where spring frosts could be dangerous. Frozen plants will defrost slowly in shade, avoiding the damage caused by rapid thawing in sun.

Damp shade does attract slugs and snails, but mites, aphids, and other pests proliferate more freely in sunny conditions.

▲ MOISTURE IN THE AIR
*Cool, humid shade in a site that is sheltered
from warm, drying summer winds makes
an ideal environment for ferns.*

◄ RETAINING MOISTURE
*Light shade shields soil from direct sun to
help meet the needs of moisture-loving plants.*

DESIGN CONSIDERATIONS

The color palette formed by shade-loving plants lends itself to the creation of subtle plantings that combine a hundred shades of blue, gray, green, and gold. Foliage forms and surface textures that contrast and harmonize invariably outlast the flowering period of shade-loving plants and can be woven into a design to help ensure a prolonged season of interest in the garden.

While themes that rely on variations in plant shape and habit may, at first, seem less dramatic than highly colored plants in bright sun, they can be just as satisfying and are certainly no less beautiful. Shade-loving plants range in height from low-growing groundcover such as sweet woodruff (*Galium*) to the showy grandeur of rhododendrons, lending themselves to layered, flowing compositions with strong focal points and a sense of perspective.

The hot, dazzling colors that are typically associated with many sun-loving plants are comparatively rare in the blooms of shade-bearers, many of which are endowed with a soft spectrum of mostly pastel colors that bring cool luminosity to even the darkest spot. The effectiveness of this type of planting can be enhanced by the use of foliage plants (*see pp.14–15*) whose leaves are marbled, striped, or splashed in shades of white, cream, and gold.

OVERHANGING BRANCHES

If a neighbor's tree casts undesirable shade across your garden, first try friendly consultation with the owner to obtain his or her permission to cut back the offending branches. Should this approach fail, the law may allow you to prune back to a line drawn vertically upward from the boundary of your property. The prunings may be considered your neighbor's property, so return or dispose of them with the owner's permission.

TYPES OF SHADE

THE SHADE IN YOUR GARDEN will often prove to be a combination of several shade types that vary in duration. Shade changes throughout each day as the sun crosses the sky, and by season because the trajectory of the winter sun is lower – markedly so at high latitudes – than that of summer. An understanding of the particular shade type, and its permanence and density, is invaluable when choosing plants that thrive in the light conditions of any given garden site.

LIGHT AND DAPPLED SHADE

The two easiest shade conditions in which to raise plants are light and dappled shade. Even plants that are normally grown in sun may thrive in these types of shade, although they can become leggy as their stems grow tall in search of light.

Light shade is the type of permanent shade that is cast by a building or wall on sites that are otherwise open to the sky. It also occurs at woodland edges or at the margins of a tree canopy. The overall effect of light shade is most marked in winter, when plants are dormant or quiescent, but it is reduced merely to the absence of direct sunlight in the growing season, when the sun is higher in the sky.

This type of shade is a positive advantage in warm climates, where the combination of sun and shelter can raise summer temperatures excessively.

Shade that occurs beneath deciduous vegetation will be dappled, forming a moving patchwork of varying intensities of shade that changes with the sun's daily course. Seasonal variations tend to be dramatic, with pronounced shade when trees are in full leaf, but less marked effects when low winter light slants beneath the trees or through a canopy of open branches. Many spring-flowering plants have adapted to this regime, completing their flowering season before the canopy closes over and reduces the light.

PROVIDING A
SUN SCREEN
Light shade at
the margins of an
overhead canopy
provides ideal
conditions for plants
such as impatiens
that may scorch and
fade in direct sun.

◄ PARTIAL SHADE
As the sun moves across the sky, shade progresses across this border. It receives more than six hours of sun each day at the height of summer, compared with two hours in winter.

▼ DAPPLED SHADE
Beneath a canopy of deciduous trees, dappled shade varies in intensity during the day and through each season.

PARTIAL SHADE

As the sun moves across the sky, a site with partial or part-day shade may receive between two and six hours of direct sun daily. This situation is ideal for plants that tolerate sun but little shade. In fact, only the most committed sun-loving plants fail to thrive in such conditions. The distinct advantage of partial shade is that it may alleviate the burning effects of midday or afternoon sun. This protection from scorch is most desirable at low latitudes; the sun's

> Many spring-flowering plants bloom before the tree canopy closes over

heat and light become more intense the nearer the equator. Even in cool climates, you should not overlook the value of afternoon shade in your garden during high summer. Morning shade maintains the cool nighttime air that is enjoyed by shade-loving plants, but if it is succeeded by direct afternoon sun, these plants can be subjected to an extreme rise in temperature with which few of them are able to cope.

DEEP SHADE

This type of shade occurs beneath dense, evergreen trees or shrubs, at the base of high walls, or in passageways that run between tall buildings and may be near-permanent if little or no direct sunlight strikes the site. Where plants are grown in the deep shade cast by trees or shrub cover, they may also need to cope with poor, dry soil (*see facing page*).

A planting in deep shade needs more thoughtful planning than those in lighter types of shade, but there are several ways to help improve the planting conditions. First, the plants selected need to be shade-demanding, rather than simply shade-tolerant. These are plants that, in nature, inhabit the woodland floor or other shady niches. The soil in a deciduous or mixed woodland tends to be rich in organic

PLANTING BENEATH A CANOPY
This varied planting lightens up an area of moist soil shaded by trees in full leaf. In the foreground, variegated irises thrive in the higher light levels bordering the canopy.

matter, thanks to the annual leaf fall, and is, consequently, well-aerated and moisture-retentive. Mimic these conditions by adding organic matter to the soil when planting (*see p.48*) and by applying a layer of mulch (*see p.50*) annually in spring. Site plants at least 18in/45cm away from the base of walls to lessen the effects of rain shadow – an area of sheltered ground that receives less rain than an open site.

A thick organic mulch in spring helps alleviate dry conditions

You can increase ambient light levels by painting surrounding walls with light-reflective colors and by using mirrors and pale-colored paving or gravel. An unplanted water feature (aquatic plants need sun), especially one where water is constantly moving, such as a bubble or wall fountain, will also contribute a little sparkle and reflect light in a shady site.

DRY SHADE

The most difficult garden situation for gardeners and plants alike is that of dry shade, which occurs in the rain shadow of walls and beneath the canopy of dense or evergreen foliage, especially where shallow-rooting trees and shrubs are taking all the moisture. The cool, sheltered conditions found in most shady sites reduce moisture loss from the soil and leaf surfaces, but if rain shadows are present, then the soil cannot be fully replenished by rainfall. The bold foliage produced by many shade-loving plants to maximize the available light contributes to the problem, since more water is lost from large leaves.

Relatively few plants are able to thrive in dry shade, which restricts the scope of planting designs, so it really helps to improve the dry soil. Add organic matter at planting time, and apply a moisture-retentive mulch to damp soil in early spring each year. Where shallow roots cause dry conditions, you can line planting holes with a perforated sheet of plastic to conserve moisture in the short term.

▲ DAMP AND THRIVING
Damp shade provides an ideal site for Ajuga reptans *and* Cardamine pratensis, *which occur naturally in damp, shady niches.*

▼ TESTING THE LIMITS
While it is one of the most problematical of sites, deep, dry shade is tolerated by a small range of plants, including useful groundcover perennials such as this comfrey.

FOLIAGE PLANTS FOR SHADE

Pʟᴀɴᴛɪɴɢs that make the most of the subtle variations in form, texture, and color of foliage are the mainstays of shade gardening. Foliage offers interest throughout the growing season – year-round for evergreens – and the beauties of foliage can easily equal the often short-lived interest of flowers. Foliage plants can prove useful as well as beautiful when used as weed-smothering groundcover or, as with variegated plants, if used to brighten shady corners.

FORM AND FUNCTION

The diverse sizes, forms, and textures that make the foliage of shade-loving plants so satisfying provide an increased leaf-surface area that allows the plants to make the most of the low levels of available light. For example, many ferns have numerous

Spreading foliage and large leaves capture the most light

tiny, divided leaflets, while hostas produce broad, flat leaves. Each leaf borne on the arching stems of Solomon's seal (*Polygonatum*) is positioned at an angle where it can receive maximum sunlight.

▲ FOLIAGE GROUNDCOVER
Here, the variegated form of goutweed (Aegopodium podagraria) *provides a light-reflecting carpet at the base of a grouping in dappled shade.*

◀ LAYERED EFFECTS
The coarse leaves of comfrey contrast attractively with those of variegated elder (Sambucus), *while honeysuckle lends height to the design.*

▲ ATTRACTIVE ASSOCIATIONS
*Even plants grown primarily for their blooms
(here,* Geranium tuberosum *and* Tulipa greigii*)
can form pleasing foliage compositions that
provide interest after the plants have flowered.*

◄ CONTRASTING FORM AND TEXTURE
*Shade-loving foliage plants offer a variety of
form, color, and variegation that provide the
perfect foil for other textures in a shady
border or container garden in a courtyard.*

COLORED FOLIAGE

Splashes, spots, and marbling in tints
of white, cream, or gold are invaluable
for providing highlights in shade; pale
colors can appear almost luminous. Bear
in mind, though, that variegated areas on
a leaf lack chlorophyll, the green pigment
plants use as part of the food-making
process to capture energy from sunlight.
The reduced area of green in the leaves
makes variegated plants less vigorous
than their all-green counterparts. As a
result, many variegated plants, especially
ivies (*Hedera*), lose their variegation in
deep shade and their leaves revert to all
green. The reduced vigor of variegated
plants can be a positive advantage in the
garden, especially if their green-leaved
counterparts are known to be rampant,
as with goutweed and periwinkle.

LEAF INTEREST FOR SHADE

EVERGREEN FOLIAGE

Ajuga reptans
Bergenia many
Euphorbia amygdaloides var. *robbiae*
Ferns most
Hedera (Ivies)
Ilex (Holly) many
Pachysandra terminalis
Pyracantha (Firethorn)
Ruscus (Broom)
Sarcococca (Christmas box)
Vinca (Periwinkle) most
Viola (Violets)

VARIEGATED FOLIAGE

Light to moderate shade
Cyclamen hederifolium, Euonymus fortunei
cultivars, *Hedera helix* many, *Hosta* many

Moderate shade
Convallaria majalis 'Albostriata', *Lunaria
annua* 'Variegata', *Polygonatum* x *hybridum*
'Striatum', *Tolmiea menziesii* 'Taff's Gold'

Moderate to deep shade
Ajuga reptans cultivars, *Asarum hartwegii,
Aucuba japonica, Brunnera macrophylla,
Fatsia japonica,* Lamium

FLOWERING PLANTS FOR SHADE

PLANTS THAT FLOWER WELL in shade offer a subtle color palette that consists of luminous shades of yellow, white, cream, pale pinks and purples, and cool blues. This range of colors is shown off at its well-preserved best when protected from the bleaching effects of the sun and is much enhanced where the soft hues appear to glow against a lush backdrop of sumptuous, shade-loving foliage accompanied by cool, still air that may be perfumed by fragrant flowers.

MIXED PLANTINGS

Planning mixed designs to make the most of a range of ornamental features for each season is essential for year-round interest. The most successful flowering plants for shady sites are those that occur naturally in shade, along with the cultivars bred or selected from these species. Shade-lovers usually bloom between late winter and early summer, before the tree canopy closes over. Light levels reduce dramatically once the trees are in leaf, so plants that produce

Many natives of woodland and forest flower in spring

flowers later in the year. Those that offer attractive fruits, fine foliage, or autumn color become all the more valuable.

A MIX OF ORNAMENTAL FEATURES
Ajugas provide a mantle of color between spring and early summer. The foliage later provides a ground-covering foil for the elegant leaves and summer flowers of hostas.

▲ SPRING-FLOWERING WOODLANDERS
The deeply colored flowers of forget-me-nots and lungworts make a glorious association in a woodland setting in spring.

◄ EXTENDING THE SEASON OF INTEREST
As English bluebells and trilliums fade, the architectural foliage and summer flowers of Rodgersia aesculifolia *come into their own.*

PROLONGING FLOWERING

Plants that are truly shade-demanding invariably bloom well and for long periods in shade, whereas those that merely tolerate shade may prove reluctant to bloom in low levels of light. Annuals and rapid-growing climbers, in particular, are often more successful when given an application of a balanced, slow-release fertilizer in spring. If the flowers are still sparse, however, a high-potassium fertilizer such as tomato food, applied at the manufacturer's recommended rate, helps encourage the production of flowers.

PLANTS WITH ADDED VALUE

LONG-LASTING FLOWERS

Anemone x *hybrida* (Japanese anemones)
Begonia semperflorens, B. coccinea
Digitalis (Foxgloves)
Hosta most
Impatiens
Lamium most
Lonicera periclymenum
Meconopsis cambrica (Welsh poppy)
Nicotiana sylvestris, N. x *sanderae* cultivars, *N.* 'Lime Green' (Flowering tobacco)
Polemonium (Jacob's ladder)

MULTIPLE SEASONS OF INTEREST

Arum italicum Spring flowers, good winter foliage, orange berries in autumn.
Astilbe Fine foliage, summer flowers, dry flowerheads through autumn and winter.
Cyclamen hederifolium Autumn flowers, good winter groundcover, marbled leaves.
Hosta Excellent foliage, good groundcover, with fragrant, mid- to late summer flowers.
Liriope muscari Evergreen, good groundcover, autumn flowers, tolerant of dry shade.
Pyracantha Evergreen foliage, spring flowers, colorful, winter-persistent berries.

PLANTS FOR SPRING

As THE DAYS LENGTHEN with the onset of spring, anticipation in the shade garden increases as new buds break to reveal the lush greens and bright tints of emergent foliage – especially so with the unfurling croziers of ferns, which are often beautifully shaded in tones of pink or chestnut brown. Spring-flowering perennials, bulbs, and shrubs add highlights of jewel-bright colors, first to bare earth and branches and later, as spring progresses, to the textures and hues of foliage.

PLANNING AHEAD

Spring is undoubtedly the easiest season to plan for. Given the range of suitable plants, it can be difficult to resist filling a site entirely with spring-flowering species, leaving little space for plants that are at their best later in the year. In gardens with acid soil, the temptation to mass camellias or rhododendrons together, where space permits, is particularly hard to resist.

To avoid inadvertently creating gaps or dull areas in your planting design as spring plants fade, be sure to site spring-flowering plants among others that will take their place as the seasons progress.

SPRING COLORS
Daffodils add color to a mantle of fresh epimedium leaves that come into their own glory a little later in the season.

CATCHING THE EARLY LIGHT
In dappled shade beneath deciduous trees, spring-flowering bulbs such as the trout lily (Erythronium revolutum) *provide color before the canopy closes over and reduces the light.*

PLANT AND PROTECT

Few sights are more glorious in early spring than carpets of snowdrops, winter aconites, or anemones. The most pleasing effects can be achieved if bulbs and perennials are planted in loose drifts. Do this by scattering bulbs randomly, then planting them where they fall. Similarly,

> Use naturalistic drifts to copy the way that plants grow in the wild

group perennials in odd numbers of three, five, or seven, taking care to avoid block plantings of geometric shapes. Autumn is the time to plant spring bulbs. To get the best effect from your spring display, site them where the dappled sunlight strikes the earth in autumn.

Spring signals the emergence of slugs and snails – a shade plant's worst enemies. Take action to reduce populations (*see p.52*) and choose plants that have a good resistance to these pests (*see p.21*).

GOOD ASSOCIATIONS

EARLY SPRING BULBS
Anemone blanda
Eranthis hyemalis (Winter aconites)
Galanthus (Snowdrops)

EARLY SPRING PERENNIALS
Anemone nemorosa (Wood anemones)
Bergenia
Helleborus (Hellebores)
Primula (Primroses)
Pulmonaria (Lungworts)

MID- TO LATE SPRING BULBS
Arum italicum 'Marmoratum'
Erythronium most
Hyacinthoides (English and Spanish Bluebells)
Leucojum vernum (Spring snowflake)
Scilla siberica (Squills)

MID- TO LATE SPRING PERENNIALS
Brunnera
Chelidonium majus 'Flore Pleno'
Epimedium
Geranium phaeum
Lamium maculatum
Trillium

PLANTS FOR SUMMER

O NCE THE SPRING flowers are over, companion summer plants begin to assume their full beauty in the cool, moist, equable conditions that shade can provide. Most of these will be plants grown for their foliage, set out to display their own individual attractions as well as to provide a lush backdrop to the precious summer jewels of those plants that do flower through the summer months. Careful selection – and a little manipulation – will make the most of their display.

REPAYING YOUR CHOICE

Compared with the numerous shade-loving plants that flower in spring, the choice of summer-flowering species is limited. Try to choose plants that are noted for their long blooming period or that offer good value during the summer. *Clematis tangutica* produces plenty of bright yellow flowers

SUMMER INTEREST

Ferns (here Dryopteris) *and* Hosta *'Fortunei Aureomarginata' look good from early summer. The foliage is enhanced by the hosta's midsummer spires of mauve bells.*

over mid- to late summer, followed by fluffy seedheads that extend interest beyond the flowering period. In terms of foliage, ferns provide many months of beauty, from the unfurling croziers in midspring to the play of light on their graceful fronds through summer. Hostas also offer long seasons of foliage, while some perennials, annuals, and biennials more than repay time spent in their selection and placement. Flowering tobaccos (*Nicotiana*), some of which carry an evening scent, and Japanese anemones (*Anemone* x *hybrida*) are valued for their long flowering periods in summer.

ONGOING BLOOMS
*This grouping of
Japanese anemones
(Anemone × hybrida),
astrantias, and
lavatera will provide
a display of flowers
over many months
in summer.*

ENCOURAGING THE DISPLAY

Several techniques can prolong a flowering display in shade. Deadheading encourages more flowers in some plants, especially if it is followed by an application of balanced fertilizer. Some shade-loving annuals can be sown in autumn or spring, so that the autumn-sown seeds flower in early summer and will be followed on by the spring sowings. Biennials such as foxgloves flower in early summer if sown in late spring in the previous year, but they may bloom later the same year if sown under glass in late winter or early spring.

VALUABLE PLANTS FOR SUMMER

GOOD FOLIAGE

Ajuga reptans
Alchemilla most
Astilbe
Ferns most
Hosta most
Kirengeshoma palmata
Lamium
Rodgersia
Shortia galacifolia
Vancouveria hexandra
Vinca (Periwinkles)

SLUG-RESISTANT PLANTS

Aconitum (Monkshood)
Actaea
Astilbe most
Begonia grandis subsp. *evansiana*
Brunnera macrophylla
Ajuga (Bugles)
Digitalis (Foxgloves) most
Epimedium
Galium odoratum (Sweet woodruff)
Helleborus (Hellebores)
Polemonium (Jacob's ladder)

AUTUMN AND WINTER INTEREST

As summer turns to autumn, there are fewer flowers to be had, and attention turns to other ornamental features to decorate the garden. In autumn, plants with good foliage color assume great importance, and fruits, berries, and dry seedheads come into their own, many persisting into winter and looking most striking when rimed with hoarfrost. In winter, the stark outlines of leafless trees and shrubs stand out in anticipation of the first of the new season's spring bulbs.

MAKING AUTUMN GLOW

As the growing season comes to a close, the few plants that offer autumn flowers in shade are all the more valued and deserve to be given prominence. The swaths of color created by *Cyclamen hederifolium* are followed by silver-marbled leaves that make a dense carpet even in dry soil. Position *Iris foetidissima* where its glossy, bright orange seeds can be seen at close quarters, perhaps offset by the tight violet-mauve flower spikes of *Liriope muscari*; both thrive in dry shade. Leave the dry seedheads of astilbes and honesty to enhance your autumn display, together with colorful grasses such as *Hakonechloa macra* 'Aureola'. Many berrying plants are at their best in autumn, from the orange spikes of arums and red-fruited actaeas to

> Take advantage of seedheads, berries, and good autumn color

the arching branches of cotoneasters and pyracanthas. Set these plants against the autumn foliage provided by *Amelanchier, Enkianthus, Fothergilla,* and *Hamamelis.*

► AUTUMN CAMEO
The heavily veined leaves of Rodgersia pinnata *turn to warm shades of red and brown in autumn.*

▼STRIKING SPIKES
The violet-mauve spikes of lilyturf (Liriope muscari) *introduce color in areas of dry shade.*

WINTER GOLD
The elegant, vase-shaped branch framework of a witch hazel (Hamamelis) *is spangled with spidery yellow flowers in late winter, making it an ideal companion for late winter bulbs.*

LASTING THROUGH WINTER

During the dull winter months, interest in the shady garden is maintained by winter-persistent berries on shrubs and trees and the dry seedheads of perennials and grasses that have been left in place during the autumn cleanup. Some of the ferns, such as *Onoclea sensibilis* and *Osmunda regalis*, will continue to display their dark, fertile fronds, while evergreens, such as the variegated forms of *Aucuba japonica* and *Euonymus fortunei*, will offer gleams of color in the winter landscape.

The stark architectural outlines of bare branches of shrubs such as *Aralia* and *Hamamelis* are at their elegant best in winter. Their open branchwork lets through valuable light for drifts of winter aconites or snowdrops (*Galanthus*), the late winter bulbs that herald the return of spring and signal a new beginning to the cycle of the seasons.

LATE-SEASON INTEREST

AUTUMN FLOWERS
Cimicifuga simplex
Gentiana asclepiadea
Hydrangea paniculata, *H. quercifolia*, *H. serrata*
Kirengeshoma palmata
Liriope muscari
Tricyrtis formosana, *T. hirta*

AUTUMN AND WINTER FRUITS
Ilex (Hollies)
Skimmia
Symphoricarpos (Snowberry)
Viburnum

LATE WINTER FLOWERS
Cornus mas
Garrya elliptica
Hamamelis (Witch hazel)
Mahonia
Sarcococca (Christmas box)

PLANTING PLANS FOR SHADE

SHADY BORDERS

WHEN PLANNING any planting design, the gardener's aim is to produce as long a season of interest as possible. In sun, this may be achieved simply by choosing long-flowering plants, whereas in shade, prolonged interest usually relies more on variations in foliage form, color, and texture. Imaginative arrangements of foliage can be pleasing in their own right and also provide a long-lasting backdrop to set off seasonal blooms.

USING GOLDEN FOLIAGE

The use of golden-leaved plants is a clever way of introducing color variation in a shady border, adding brightness and warmth to a palette that might otherwise consist mainly of greens in various hues and tints. Many golden-leaved plants can scorch when grown in full light and so are displayed to their best advantage if protected with some shade, especially during the hottest hours of the day.

Plants with white, cream, or golden variegation on their leaves also have the positively beneficial effect of lending an impression of light, which helps brighten dark or gloomy corners in a border. Bear in mind, however, that a few variegated plants, notably the ivies, often need higher light levels than their more shade-tolerant, green-leaved forms to develop their patterns of variegation fully.

LIGHT RELIEF
Hot midday sun frequently scorches the foliage of golden-leaved plants, and many need at least part-day shade to produce their best effects.

◀ BRIGHT BORDER *Narrow, shaded beds alongside buildings need not be dull.*

PLAN FOR A SHADY BORDER

This shady border in midsummer shows the beautiful effects that can be achieved with a very limited color palette – mostly greens and golds, with seasonal splashes of blue (*Brunnera macrophylla* 'Dawson's White') and rich yellow (*Meconopsis cambrica*). Sculptural plants, such as angelica, hostas, and euphorbia, provide height and a seasonal series of focal points, with lower layers of alchemilla and ajuga covering the ground at their feet.

PLANTING PLAN

1   3 *Hosta* 'Birchwood Parky's Gold', 30in/75cm apart
2   5 *Meconopsis cambrica*, 10in/25cm apart
3   3 *Alchemilla mollis*, 30in/75cm apart
4   5 *Lunaria annua* 'Variegata', 12in/30cm apart
5   1 *Euphorbia characias* subsp. *wulfenii*, spread 4ft/1.2m
6   3 *Ajuga reptans* 'Variegata' 20in/50cm apart
7   1 *Hedera helix* 'Buttercup', 7ft/2.2m high on wall
8   3 *Hakonechloa macra* 'Aureola', 16in/40cm apart
9   3 *Brunnera macrophylla* 'Dawson's White', 24in/60cm apart
10   1 *Angelica archangelica*, spread 4ft/1.2m
11   3 *Hosta* 'Gold Standard', 30in/75cm apart

4ft/1.2m

13ft/4m

Euphorbia characias subsp. *wulfenii* contributes elegant evergreen foliage, with sculptural flowerheads in early spring.

Hosta 'Birchwood Parky's Gold' makes mounds of golden, ground-covering foliage.

MECONOPSIS CAMBRICA
A yellow-flowered perennial poppy blooming throughout summer. Self-sows randomly, giving an informal effect.

Alchemilla mollis, a stalwart self-seeding perennial that can be controlled by pulling up unwanted seedlings.

ANGELICA ARCHANGELICA is a statuesque biennial with large clusters of yellow-green flowers in summer. It may self-sow, or you can collect the seeds when ripe.

MORE CHOICES

SCULPTURAL PLANTS

Aesculus parviflora
Angelica gigas
Aralia elata
x Fatshedera lizei
Kirengeshoma palmata
Matteuccia struthiopteris
Rheum palmatum
Rodgersia pinnata
Sambucus nigra 'Laciniata',
  S. racemosa 'Plumosa Aurea'

GROUNDCOVERS

Alchemilla alpina
Pachyphragma macrophyllum
Pachysandra terminalis
Pulmonaria many
Sanguinaria canadensis
  'Plena'
Saxifraga x urbium
Tellima grandiflora
Tiarella cordifolia
Waldsteinia ternata

Hedera helix 'Buttercup' is a moderately vigorous ivy ideal for shady walls, with light green leaves that brighten to yellow where sunlight falls on them.

Lunaria annua 'Variegata' is a self-seeding annual or biennial honesty with red-purple flowers in spring followed by flat, silvery seedpods.

Hosta 'Gold Standard' has heart-shaped leaves in shades of cream, yellow, and green.

Ajuga reptans 'Variegata' forms dense, year-round groundcover with blue flower spikes.

Hakonechloa macra 'Aureola' forms an elegant tuft of golden leaves.

Brunnera macrophylla 'Dawson's White' provides foliage interest after its tiny blue flowers fade in early summer.

SHADY CITY GARDENS

A N ENCLOSED CITY GARDEN should never be regarded as a damp, dank space with which nothing can be done. Look on it instead as an opportunity to create a cool haven from the noise, heat, and dust of the city. Many urban gardens have a strong geometric outline that provides the perfect setting for the elegant formality of a courtyard garden that is softened by lush foliage, illuminated by summer flowers, and permeated with rich and sensual scents.

A COURTYARD GARDEN

An attractive paved area with plants in containers is an ideal solution for city gardens where soil may be altogether absent or of poor quality, and the shelter and warmth of an enclosed urban space will almost certainly increase the range of plants that you can grow. Containers can be filled with specific soil mix to suit the individual requirements of each plant. The range of containers is extensive, and choosing them for their sculptural qualities will make them a feature in their own right. All but the very largest pots can be moved around, either to make the most of available light or to provide an ever-changing series of focal points.

PRACTICAL TIPS

• Make the most of available light by painting surrounding walls with reflective white or pale-colored masonry paints.
• Choose light-colored paving slabs or gravel for paths and paved areas, and use pale gravels for top-dressing soil – this also helps keep down weeds.
• Consider installing a mirror to reflect light and create an illusion of greater space.
• Always remember that whatever the material (plastic, metal, terracotta, or other), all pots must have adequate drainage holes if the plants in them are to thrive.
• When planting up containers, use soil-based mixes for weight, stability, and superior, long-term nutrient status.

FORMAL PASSAGE
A narrow alleyway has been transformed by the introduction of elegant boxwood topiary, set off against white-painted walls that make the most of the reflection of ambient light.

◀ PERFUMED GARDEN *An enclosed space captures the fragrance of lilies and flowering tobacco.*

PLAN FOR A SHADY COURTYARD

Seen in mid- to late summer, this plan shows the potential of walls and fences for using climbing plants that enjoy shade; sun-loving plants would simply clamber to the top and flower there chiefly for your neighbors' benefit. The depth of shade in an enclosed garden varies with exposure, but the highest levels of light fall in the central area that is fully open to the sky. This part of a garden provides an ideal site for those usually sun-loving plants that often tolerate or thrive in bright shade. A mirror on the far wall amplifies the light and gives the illusion of a formal vista.

ROSA 'ALBERIC BARBIER' is a shade-tolerant, semievergreen rambling rose bearing faintly scented white flowers in summer.

Nicotiana alata 'Lime Green', an annual with unusually colored summer blooms that appear to glow in shade.

Clematis 'Alba Luxurians' has gray-green foliage and small, bell-shaped white flowers from summer to autumn.

MORE CHOICES

FRAGRANT PLANTS

Choisya ternata
Convallaria majalis
Cyclamen hederifolium
Nicotiana sylvestris
Lonicera periclymenum
Rhododendron molle subsp.
  japonicum, R. luteum
Sarcococca most
Viburnum many
Viola odorata

FOR CONTAINERS

Aucuba japonica
  'Crotonifolia'
Begonia grandis
Fargesia nitida
Hydrangea serrata
  'Bluebird'
Osmanthus × burkwoodii
Pieris japonica 'Little
  Heath'
Prunus lusitanica
Viburnum carlesii

PLANTING PLAN

1 1 *Clematis* 'Alba Luxurians',
   spread 5ft/1.5m
2 1 *Rosa* 'Albéric Barbier', spread 10ft/3m
3 7 *Nicotiana alata* 'Lime Green',
   10in/25cm apart
4 3 *Anemone* x *hybrida* 'Honorine
   Jobert', 30in/75cm apart
5 1 *Hosta* 'Frances Williams', spread 3ft/1m
6 1 *Buxus sempervirens* 'Suffruticosa',
   in container; also used as low hedging
7 4 *Hydrangea quercifolia*, in containers
8 1 *Rosa* 'New Dawn', spread 8ft/2.5m
9 1 *Clematis rehderiana*, spread 10ft/3m

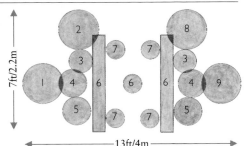

7ft/2.2m

13ft/4m

Hydrangea quercifolia bears cone-shaped white flowerheads in summer, followed by attractive autumn tints.

'New Dawn' is a healthy, vigorous rose bearing multiple flushes of fragrant pink flowers during summer.

ANEMONE x *HYBRIDA*
'HONORINE JOBERT'
*has cup-shaped, glowing
white flowers amid clumps
of pretty foliage, borne
in long succession from
midsummer onward.*

Buxus sempervirens
'Suffruticosa' is the
perfect dwarf boxwood
for border edging
or topiary.

Clematis rehderiana
produces tubular, bell-
shaped yellow flowers
with a distinct cowslip
scent in midsummer
and autumn.

Hosta 'Frances Williams'
forms substantial
mounds of thick-
textured, puckered, blue-
green leaves with yellow
variegation, and scented
summer flowers.

PLANTING UNDER TREES

FEW GARDENS ARE LARGE ENOUGH to accommodate an extensive woodland garden, but many have a few trees. Planting beneath them can often prove difficult, because venturing roots take moisture and nutrients from the soil. Some trees, though, have deep taproots, rather than surface roots. If you are fortunate in having such trees, or choose new trees carefully, underplanting can be more exciting and will certainly end up being more successful than planting grass.

LETTING IN MORE LIGHT

Sometimes, it is desirable to increase the light levels beneath trees, especially where you intend to introduce extensive underplanting. Letting in more light is best done by lifting or thinning the canopy (*see below*).

If trees and their lower branches are small enough for this to be carried out by hand with a bow saw, you can safely tackle the task yourself. With mature trees and heavy, dense branchwork, however, removing large branches is an extremely dangerous job that should be left to a professional arborist.

TREE SURGERY

Poor or careless tree surgery can be expensive to rectify and may even result in a tree being lost altogether. Therefore, when looking for an arborist (tree surgeon), contact recommended professionals and ask for site visits and estimates before any work is carried out. Obtain assurance that all felled wood will be removed from the site if you wish, and that any liability for damage or compensation claims is their, not your, responsibility.

Height of the clear trunk is increased

CROWN LIFTING
Crown lifting is when the lower branches of a tree are removed to allow easy access beneath or to admit more light.

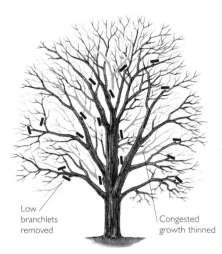

Low branchlets removed

Congested growth thinned

CROWN THINNING
Crown thinning involves the removal of up to one-third of the growth on main branches to allow more light through the tree's canopy.

◀ A RAISED CANOPY *Tall-trunked trees allow spring flowers to make a colorful underplanting.*

CREATING A SHADY NOOK

A tree is often among the first additions to be considered in a new garden, and with careful choice you can greatly increase the scope for attractive underplanting. Deep-rooting deciduous trees with slender, bare trunks and light, airy canopies allow the plants below to thrive without too much competition from tree roots. A flowering tree with plants in flower below (as here, in early summer) creates a superb focal point.

STYRAX JAPONICUS
A deep-rooting small tree of light, airy habit, with summer flowers and good autumn color. Good for small gardens and underplanting.

Iris sibirica 'Lady of Quality' forms attractive clumps of narrow, fresh green leaves and glowing blue-violet flowers in early summer.

Bergenia purpurascens has purple-red flowers in spring. The leathery dark green leaves turn red-purple in winter.

Polygonatum x *hybridum* has elegant foliage and bell-shaped white flowers borne on arching stems.

Actaea alba bears white flowers in spring and summer, followed by clusters of white berries in autumn.

Primula florindae is a rosette-forming perennial with fragrant, pale yellow flowers in summer.

PLANTING PLAN

 1 3 *Iris sibirica* 'Lady of Quality', 24in/60cm apart
 2 3 *Bergenia purpurascens*, 12in/30cm apart
 3 1 *Styrax japonicus*, spread to 26ft/8m
 4 3 *Polygonatum* x *hybridum*, 12in/30cm apart
 5 3 *Primula florindae*, 30in/75cm apart
 6 3 *Actaea alba*, 24in/60cm apart
 7 3 *Aconitum* 'Ivorine', 18in/45cm apart
 8 3 *Campanula* 'Telham Beauty', 30in/75cm apart
 9 3 *Dicentra spectabilis* 'Alba', 16in/40cm apart
10 3 *Anemone sylvestris*, 20in/50cm apart
11 1 *Polystichum setiferum* Divisilobum Group, spread 20–28in/50–70cm

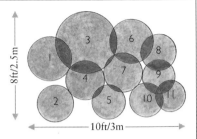

8ft/2.5m — 10ft/3m

CAMPANULA PERSICIFOLIA 'TELHAM BEAUTY' *bears luminous blue flowers over long periods from early summer, especially if regularly deadheaded.*

Dicentra spectabilis 'Alba' flowers for a longer period than the pink-flowered species.

Polystichum setiferum Divisilobum Group has finely divided, fresh green fronds that provide textural interest throughout the year.

CHOOSING TREES

Good choices for under-planting in small gardens
Acer capillipes,
  A. davidii
Betula albosinensis
Carya cordiformis
Celtis occidentalis
Cercis canadensis, especially 'Forest Pansy'
Cornus controversa,
  C. 'Eddie's White Wonder',
  C. florida, C. mas,
  C. nuttallii
Sophora japonica
Sorbus most species
Styrax obassia
Zelkova serrata

Aconitum 'Ivorine' has divided, fresh green foliage and spires of creamy flowers in early summer.

Anemone sylvestris is a spreading perennial with delicate white flowers in late spring and early summer.

PLANTING UNDER A LARGE TREE

A large, mature tree in leaf will shade a wide area of ground by mid-summer; use shrubs to give height and structure to planting below, interplanted with perennials that will really thrive in the double shade of the tree canopy and the larger plants. The dappled shade cast by this stately oak (*Quercus alba*) is accentuated by the choice of mainly white-flowered plants growing underneath, shown here as summer turns to autumn.

PLANTING PLAN

 1 3 *Tricyrtis hirta*, 24in/60cm apart
 2 1 *Hydrangea paniculata* 'Grandiflora', spread 8ft/2.5m
 3 3 *Actaea rubra*, 12in/30cm apart
 4 1 *Quercus alba*, spread to 80ft/25m
 5 3 *Gentiana asclepiadea*, 18in/45cm apart
 6 3 *Phegopteris connectilis*, 20in/50cm apart
 7 3 *Vancouveria hexandra*, 16in/40cm apart
 8 3 *Nicotiana sylvestris*, 24in/60cm apart
 9 3 *Lilium martagon*, 12in/30cm apart
10 1 *Fothergilla major*, spread 6ft/2m
11 3 *Hakonechloa macra* 'Aureola', 16in/40cm apart

8ft/2.5m

13ft/4m

Gentiana asclepiadea is a clump-forming perennial with rich blue or white, bell-shaped flowers in late summer and autumn.

HYDRANGEA PANICULATA 'GRANDIFLORA' *is a deciduous shrub with large, white flowerheads borne in late summer, and good color in autumn.*

Tricyrtis hirta spreads by rhizomes. An unusual perennial, it bears funnel-shaped, white flowers with purple spots in autumn.

NICOTIANA SYLVESTRIS
*is a robust woodland annual
bearing large panicles of
very fragrant white flowers
throughout summer.*

MORE CHOICES

SHRUBS AND TREES

*Amelanchier canadensis,
  A. laevis, A. lamarckii*
*Callicarpa bodinieri,
  C. dichotoma*
Cornus mas
Enkianthus most
Mahonia aquifolium
Pyracantha most
Rhododendron
Viburnum x *burkwoodii*

GROUNDCOVER

*Alchemilla alpina,
  A. conjuncta*
Arctostaphylos uva-ursi
Blechnum penna-marina
Brunnera macrophylla
Euphorbia amygdaloides
  var. *robbiae*
Gaultheria mucronata
Geranium macrorrhizum
Maianthemum bifolium

Quercus alba is a large,
deep-rooting deciduous
tree that casts ideal
dappled shade for
plants below.

Lilium martagon, a bulbous
perennial with pink to
purple-red turkscap flowers
in early summer.

Actaea rubra.has spires
of white flowers in early
summer, followed by glossy
red berries in autumn.

Fothergilla major is a
deciduous shrub with
stunning autumn color
and scented white bottle-
brush flowers in spring.

*Hakonechloa
macra* 'Aureola'
is a clump-forming
woodland grass
with good
autumn color.

*Phegopteris
connectilis* spreads
by rhizomes. The
delicate, fresh
green fronds of
this fern make
good ground-
cover throughout
the season.

Vancouveria hexandra is a
creeping groundcover perennial
with lobed, bright green leaves
and tiny white flowers in early summer.

DAMP SHADE

MANY GARDENS POSSESS A DAMP, shady corner, often inherited from previous owners and frequently uninspiring, but with thoughtful planting it can become an admirable feature in its own right. Although often in permanent shade, it may be graduated from light to deep, or dappled, and the cool and humid conditions will suit a wide range of shade- and moisture-loving plants. In most cases, the only major improvement needed is the incorporation of organic matter before planting and an annual mulch or feed to maintain soil fertility. For decorative interest and atmosphere, add a small water feature.

PROBLEM-SOLVING PLANTS

To avoid having to do too much work in damp, shady areas and compacting the soil, consider a plan that is based on low-maintenance groundcover plants. Ivies and deadnettles (*Lamium*) make superb cover for "problem" sites, tolerating both damp and dry shade and poor soil. Ivies, together with climbing hydrangeas, are also the ideal choice for permanently shaded walls and fences. Most groundcover plants spread quickly by means of creeping roots or rooting stems. You can mulch between plants while they are small (*see p.48*) to suppress weed growth between them until they grow and knit together.

Good preparation is crucial for a successful groundcover. If not done properly, it becomes a tangled mat that is hopelessly intertwined with weeds, which are extremely difficult to eradicate without damage to ornamental plants. The most important part of preparation, therefore, is to clear the ground thoroughly of all weeds, especially perennial ones such as quack grass. Spraying with a systemic weedkiller is the quickest method. If you don't wish to use chemicals, weeds can be removed by hand when digging over or, if you are planning well ahead, covered with black plastic or old carpet.

LIGHTENING THE WORKLOAD
This low-maintenance planting uses closely planted groundcovers as a horizontal foil for the vertical element provided by ivy scrambling over an old tree trunk. Bare soil is mulched to suppress weeds.

◀ MOISTURE LOVERS *Calla lilies provide focal points in a streamside setting in shade.*

PLAN FOR DAMP SHADE

In this design for a damp, shady spot, shade is cast by high adjacent walls and by the airy-leaved birch tree, although lightened by the birch's bright white trunk. The back wall is clothed with climbing hydrangea, which provides a strong vertical element to the design of the planting and an interesting winter framework. A carpet of groundcovers is used as a foil for a succession of flowers that change with the seasons.

DIGITALIS PURPUREA 'ALBA'
A biennial with spires of creamy white flowers, whose season can be prolonged with autumn and spring sowings.

Brunnera macrophylla offers sprays of small, pure blue flowers in spring and then beautifully textured leaves that enlarge after flowering.

Betula ermanii 'Grayswood Hill' is an elegant, airy tree with glowing, pure white bark. It casts light, dappled shade.

Helleborus niger 'Potter's Wheel' has bowl-shaped, green-eyed white flowers in late winter. Remove last year's leaves to display flowers to best effect.

HEDERA HELIX 'GLACIER'
forms a ground-covering carpet of gray-green leaves marbled with silver-gray. Plant at the margins of the shade-casting canopy.

Helleborus x *hybridus* 'Ballard's Black' makes a dramatic contrast plant with its deep, dark purple flowers borne in late winter and spring.

PLANTING PLAN

1 3 *Digitalis purpurea* f. *albiflora*,
   24in/60cm apart
2 3 *Brunnera macrophylla*,
   24in/60cm apart
3 3 *Helleborus niger* 'Potter's Wheel',
   18in/45cm apart
4 1 *Betula ermanii* 'Grayswood Hill',
   spread to 40ft/12m
5 3 *Helleborus* x *hybridus* 'Ballard's Black',
   18in/45cm apart
6 3 *Hedera helix* 'Glacier', 3ft/1m apart
7 3 *Astilbe* 'Irrlicht', 20in/60cm apart
8 3 *Astrantia* 'Shaggy', 18in/45cm apart
9 3 *Pulmonaria officinalis* 'Sissinghurst
   White', 18in/45cm apart
10 1 *Hydrangea anomala* subsp. *petiolaris*,
   spread to 50ft/15m

11 3 *Epimedium grandiflorum* 'Rose
   Queen', 12in/30cm apart
12 5 *Lamium maculatum* 'Beacon Silver',
   30in/75cm apart

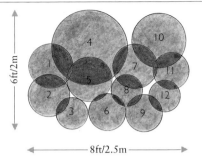

6ft/2m

8ft/2.5m

Hydrangea petiolaris produces creamy flowers in summer, set off against dark leaves that turn yellow in autumn.

Astilbe 'Irrlicht' has creamy white plumes above finely divided, dark green leaves in spring and early summer. They persist into winter.

SELF-SEEDERS

Flowering plants that may pop up randomly among groundcovers include:
Aquilegia vulgaris
Arum italicum 'Marmoratum'
Chelidonium majus
Chionodoxa forbesii
Digitalis purpurea
Geranium phaeum
Hesperis matronalis
Lunaria annua
Ornithogalum montanum
Polemonium pauciflorum
Scilla siberica
Viola odorata

Epimedium grandiflorum 'Rose Queen' produces deep bronze-purple new leaves and spurred, rose-pink flowers in spring.

Pulmonaria officinalis 'Sissinghurst White' bears white flowers in late spring, above silvery, white-spangled leaves that come into their full beauty after flowering.

Lamium maculatum 'Beacon Silver': good groundcover with clear pink flowers in summer and silver leaves. Tolerates poor, dry soils, too.

SPECIAL PLANT COLLECTIONS

Make a feature of a cool, shady spot by using it to display one of the beautiful foliage plant groups that need these conditions. Working with a restricted color palette, as with ferns, or with similar leaf shapes, as with hostas, makes it all the more fascinating – even addictive – when planning designs that associate and contrast different textures and hues. Specimens of different heights will give structure and variety to your composition.

MAKING A FEATURE OF FERNS

As a group, ferns can be fairly considered as the ultimate shade plants and could hardly be better designed for use in places where light levels are low. They tend to have been rather neglected since the early part of this century but are now, once again, being appreciated for their beauty and versatility.

In Victorian England, displays of plant collections were large and theatrical, and ferneries would be embellished by props such as moss-covered "fallen" trees, grottoes, and cascades. Such a feature is not difficult to scale down for a small garden and is fun to design and build – or you may prefer to integrate your fern collection more into the garden by introducing a few other, complementary plants among them. Use other foliage plants with sculptural qualities to create

FERN-GROWING TIPS

• A cool, humid, shady site, with a moisture-retentive, organic soil and some shelter from strong, cold, or drying winds is all that most ferns ask. Work as much organic matter into your soil before planting as you can.
• Provide shelter from wind with barrier plantings or hedges. Solid barriers can create harmful turbulence in their lee.

strong textural contrasts. Rodgersias, hostas, rheums and grasses fit this purpose well; for lower-level planting, use neat-leaved groundcovers such as *Vancouveria* and *Waldsteinia*. Introduce flower color with woodlanders, such as dicentras, *Chelidonium majus* or *Meconoposis cambrica*, which self-sow to produce beautiful natural effects.

TAKING COVER
In this courtyard garden, planting in paving crevices provides ideal cool, damp conditions at the plants' roots. Ferns that spread by rhizomes, such as Phegopteris *and* Gymnocarpium, *are eager to infiltrate paving crevices.*

◀ DISTINCTIVE FRONDS *Ferns are seen at their best when backlit by dappled sunlight.*

PLAN FOR A SMALL FERNERY

This design exploits ferns' natural diversity of form. Tall shuttlecocks of finely divided fronds, such as those of *Matteuccia*, are used in contrast with creeping, rhizomatous ferns, such as *Phegopteris*, which spread to form a verdant carpet. The color range includes many shades of green, enhanced by the spring tints of emerging croziers, a golden grass and gold-splashed hosta, and the yellow of Welsh poppies (*Meconopsis cambrica*).

PLANTING PLAN

1 3 *Meconopsis cambrica*, 10in/25cm apart
2 1 *Phegopteris connectilis*, spread 16in/50cm
3 1 *Adiantum venustum*, spread 16in/50cm
4 1 *Matteuccia struthiopteris*, spread 3ft/1m
5 1 *Athyrium niponicum* 'Pictum', spread 16in/50cm
6 3 *Carex elata* 'Aurea', 18in/45cm apart
7 1 *Asplenium scolopendrium* 'Crispum', spread 2ft/60cm
8 3 *Osmunda cinnamomea*, 2ft/60cm apart
9 1 *Polypodium vulgare* 'Cornubiense', spread 2ft/60cm
10 1 *Hosta* 'Fortunei Albomarginata', spread 30in/80cm
11 1 *Polystichum setiferum* Divisilobum Group, spread 2ft/60cm

Matteuccia struthiopteris, the ostrich fern, with arching, finely divided, pale green sterile fronds and in midsummer, central clumps of dark brown fertile fronds.

Meconopsis cambrica is a self-seeding perennial with bluish green leaves and orange or golden yellow flowers borne throughout summer.

Phegopteris connectilis is a carpet-forming fern with soft triangular fronds of pale bright green.

Adiantum venustum is a creeping fern. The fan-shaped, bright green segments are held on glossy black stalks and are bright bronze-pink as they unfurl in spring.

Athyrium niponicum 'Pictum' has finely divided fronds that are unusual in being variegated. The silver-gray frond segments complement red-purple stalks.

MORE PLANTS TO GROW WITH FERNS

Alchemilla mollis
Arum italicum 'Marmoratum'
Asarum europaeum
Bergenia
Cornus canadensis
Corydalis lutea

Dicentra spectabilis
Galium odoratum
Helleborus
Kirengeshoma palmata
Podophyllum hexandrum
Tellima grandiflora

POLYPODIUM VULGARE
'CORNUBIENSE' *is a*
vigorous, ground-covering
fern with variably divided
fronds of interesting texture.

Osmunda cinnamomea
is a deciduous shuttlecock
fern with pale blue-green
sterile fronds and upright,
central fertile fronds bearing
cinnamon-brown spores
that persist into winter.

POLYSTICHUM SETIFERUM
DIVISILOBUM GROUP *has*
shuttlecocks of soft-textured
fronds divided finely into
very narrow segments.

Carex elata 'Aurea', a creeping
golden sedge, forms clumps of
narrow, arching leaves of rich
yellow margined with green.

Asplenium scolopendrium
'Crispum' is an evergreen fern
producing shuttlecocks of strap-
shaped, glossy, bright green
fronds with wavy margins.

Hosta 'Fortunei
Albomarginata' forms
substantial mounds of large,
heart-shaped, deeply veined
leaves of olive-green with
irregular golden margins.

CARING FOR PLANTS IN SHADE

PREPARING AND PLANTING

YOUR FIRST STEP is to assess the types of shade and soil conditions on your site: then you should choose only those plants that are suited to your conditions. There is also plenty of practical help to give plants right at the start that will ensure satisfying results and less work in the future.

IMPROVING GROWING CONDITIONS

Before you buy any plants, prepare the soil well (*see p.48*), clearing weeds and improving the soil structure. Consider whether there is anything else you can do to make the site more conducive to plant growth – painting a wall white to reflect in more light, for example, or thinning existing shrubs (*see below*) so that they cast less shade on the ground. Thinning also benefits shrubs that grow in shade, letting in light and air around their branches and onto plants below. Check in a reference guide to determine the specific pruning needs of your shrubs before making cuts.

THINNING FROM THE BASE
Shrubs that form a thicket of upright or arching stems can be thinned by cutting out some main stems right at the base. Remove one in three or four in any one year, choosing the oldest. You may need loppers or a pruning saw; do not overstrain and damage pruners on thick stems.

THINNING BUSHY GROWTH
Thin shrubs with branching stems not by trimming back side branches but by cutting main stems down to a new, upright sideshoot. Don't worry if it looks awkward at first: the growth on this shoot as it becomes the new branch leader will soon make it arch over attractively.

COPPICING

Shrubs that can be cut back hard in early spring every year or two include hazel (*Corylus*), smoke bush (*Cotinus*), elder (*Sambucus*), and some dogwoods (*Cornus*) and willows (*Salix*). The extra light will increase your choice of underplanting.

◀EYE-CATCHERS *Good preparation and care help ensure that you get the very best from plants.*

PREPARING THE SITE

Preplanting preparations benefit the future health of your soil and plants. Dig over new planting areas in the season before you intend to plant to give the soil time to settle. This also allows time before planting to use a systemic weedkiller on any perennial weeds – or, remove by hand as you dig. Incorporate plenty of well-rotted organic matter; it improves the drainage and workability of clay soils and increases the nutrient content and moisture-retentiveness of light soils.

IMPROVING THE SOIL
On new ground, work in organic matter (see below) to a spade's depth when digging over. This is hard work but worthwhile, and it seldom needs to be repeated. It is sufficient to fork in organic matter into the top 3–4in/8–10cm of areas to be planted under trees and in established borders, avoiding damage to existing plants' roots.

MAKE A MULCH

The leaf fall from deciduous garden trees is a ready source of leaf mold. Prepare your own organic soil additive or mulch by raking them up and stacking in a circular cage made from chicken wire around stakes about 3ft/1m tall and apart. If shredded first, the leaves will decompose quickly and be ready to use the following spring.

MANURE
Well-rotted manure adds some nutrients and organic matter.

MUSHROOM COMPOST
Highly organic but contains lime.

COMPOST
Fine soil improver, containing some valuable nutrients.

LEAF MOLD
Low-level nutrients; makes a natural-looking mulch.

PROVIDING ACCESS

Soil structure is easily compacted when wet, leading to a shortage of oxygen at the plant roots and poor drainage. Most shade-lovers need moist soils, which makes it difficult to gain access for deadheading and other routine tasks without compacting the site. To avoid damaging soil and plants, add a platform or some stepping stones from which you can work, using natural materials such as log sections or by laying small pavers within a border; these will quickly be disguised by plant growth.

PLANTING POT-GROWN PLANTS

Plants grown in containers can be planted at any time the soil is not frozen or baked dry, but they must be watered regularly until well established. They should be planted at the same level as in their pots, but this can make them difficult to water properly because of runoff. If the water permeates only the surface layers, roots tend to grow up toward the surface to reach it, where they will be even more exposed to heat and drought. You can mound up a ring of soil around the plant that will hold water, or add a watering pipe (*right*). Drip-feed systems or seep hoses are especially convenient for groups of plants, supplying water directly to the soil surface above the root zone of each one; they are best used with a timer to avoid any unnecessary waste of water.

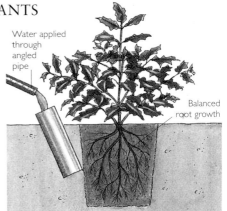

Water applied through angled pipe

Balanced root growth

REACHING THE ROOTS
Position a section of old plastic pipe at an angle to the plant so that one end is near to the root zone and the other end is open to the air at or just within the plant's canopy. Water can then be applied directly to the roots.

SPECIAL PLANTING NEEDS

Buy spring-flowering bulbs in autumn, and vice versa. Most should be planted at a depth 3–5 times their height, setting larger bulbs deeper. Tie climbers, even self-climbing ones, into supports to help them grow away. Trees, shrubs, and climbers may be sold bare-root or with their roots wrapped or bagged with a little soil mix. Buy and plant these only in autumn or spring. Autumn plantings should establish well in cool, rainy weather, but spring may be safer in cold areas. Dig a hole twice the width of the rootball and 1½ times its depth. Spread out the roots in the hole and adjust the depth so that the soil level will match the soil mark on the stem or stems. Backfill and firm in, then water and mulch (*see p.50*). Water regularly until established.

PLANTING CLIMBERS
To give a young climber more light before training it into a host shrub, train it first up a pole next to the shrub so it can grow up and over the host's branches, rather than struggling through them.

PLANTING SNOWDROPS
Snowdrops are not planted as dry bulbs but "in the green," looking rather like scallions. Firm them in gently and keep well watered; the foliage should soon perk up.

ROUTINE PLANT CARE

Keep the site weed-free and check regularly for signs of any problems caused by pests or diseases (*see p.52*). Most plants need little or no additional fertilizer in woodland soils, since the annual leaf fall recycles plant nutrients. Elsewhere, apply a balanced slow-release fertilizer in early spring to improve growth and flower production. Regular deadheading helps encourage more blooms.

FERTILIZING AND MULCHING

Apply fertilizer at the manufacturers' recommended rate, since plant roots can be damaged by applications that are too heavy. Shield any topgrowth from contact with the fertilizer to prevent damaging the leaves. Fork fertilizer in lightly, taking care not to damage shallow roots, then apply an annual mulch. Ornamental foliage plants, such as hostas, benefit from an additional liquid fertilizer during the growing season.

WOOD CHIPS

GRAVEL

HOW TO APPLY FERTILIZER
Sprinkle directly on to damp soil a little way from the plant base. Fork in lightly to avoid roots.

MULCHING GROUNDCOVER
A 2–4in/5–10cm layer of bark- or wood chips, leaf mold, or gravel between plants keeps moisture in.

PLANTING THROUGH SHEET MULCHES

Sheet mulches allow complete weed control beneath plants that grow from a single stem and help to conserve moisture and regulate soil temperature. Fiber fleeces or landscape fabric are permeable to air and water and allow fertilizer to be applied when required. Remove any perennial weeds before mulching, and lay it onto damp soil. Remember to perforate black plastic to allow the passage of water. To plant through a sheet mulch, make a cross-shaped incision in the sheet just large enough to insert a plant. Fold back the sheet corners when planting, and water well before adding a top-dressing.

FINISHING TOUCH
Top-dress sheet mulches with natural-looking materials such as cocoa shells, bark chips, or gravel for an attractive finish.

KEEPING UP APPEARANCES

In autumn, clean up herbaceous plants that are dying back, not just for neatness but for good garden hygiene; many plants will rot if overwintered with wet, decomposing material at their crowns. Cut down flowered stems and trim top growth from perennials, using pruners or scissors. Pick fallen leaves out of plants by hand, and rake up those on the ground using a spring-tine rake. Use them to make leaf mold (*see p.48*) for mulching. Some evergreen perennials, most notably epimediums and hellebores, benefit from special treatment in spring to give their best (*see right*). Do not, however, trim back the foliage of spring bulbs after flowering; the plants need to keep it until it dies naturally to build up their strength.

SHOWING OFF SPRING FLOWERS
Cut out old, dark green leaves at the base in late winter or early spring, when the emerging flowerbuds and new foliage shoots are visible.

TRIMMING
Some groundcover plants can be cut with a nylon line trimmer to remove tattered foliage. Do this in autumn or very early spring to avoid damaging any new shoots.

Plants that can be trimmed: *Euphorbia amygdaloides* var. *robbiae*, *Hypericum calycinum*, *Liriope muscari*, *Vinca major*

SUCKER REMOVAL
Suckers from roots sap a plant's energy. Trace them to their point of origin and pull them off with a sharp tug. Neaten the wound with a sharp knife to remove nearby dormant buds.

Plants prone to producing suckers: grafted plants, including *Hamamelis* cultivars, roses, and *Corylus avellana* 'Contorta'

REMOVING REVERTED SHOOTS
Cut out reverted, or all-green, shoots that appear on variegated plants, since they are more vigorous and may become dominant over variegated growth.

Plants prone to reversion: *Aralia elata* 'Variegata', *Euonymus fortunei* 'Silver Queen', *Aucuba japonica* 'Crotonifolia'

REMOVING NON-VARIEGATED SHOOTS
Remove any plain gold or cream shoots on variegated plants, since they make the plant less able to use limited light resources efficiently when grown in a shady site.

Prone to producing all cream/yellow leaves: all white-leaved plants, *Euonymus fortunei* 'Silver Queen', *E. fortunei* 'Emerald 'n' Gold'

KEEPING PLANTS HEALTHY

REGULAR INSPECTIONS of your plants, removing weeds while small and simply picking off pests or any diseased stems or leaves often prevent problems from taking hold. If problems do become severe, ask at a garden center for advice if you wish to use a chemical control, and follow the manufacturer's instructions carefully. Where possible, use organic or "natural" methods or pest-specific chemicals to avoid killing beneficial creatures that attack pests.

FRIENDS AND FOES

Shaded sites, particularly when well planted and mulched, will be cool in summer and cozy in winter, attracting all manner of creatures. Learn to identify between garden friends and foes before reaching for deterrents. Skunks, thrushes, frogs, toads, and shrews all eat slugs and insect pests but are vulnerable to garden chemicals, so if you want to encourage wildlife into the garden, do not eliminate pests too assiduously to leave beneficial creatures something to feed on. Sowbugs tend to damage seedlings under glass but are welcomed outdoors for their habit of recycling dead plant material. Aphids and caterpillars will be less common since they prefer sun, but slugs and snails (*see below*) will congregate in cool, moist sites.

MOSTLY HARMLESS
In open gardens or woodland, sowbugs live in the surface layers of soil and are primarily recyclers of organic material. They tend to harm only young seedlings.

GARDEN SNAILS
These unwelcome visitors are active in the cool of the evening and in wet weather, making holes in foliage and leaving behind slime trails which often dry to silvery deposits.

SLUGS AND SNAILS

The main enemies of plants in shade are slugs and snails. Active between spring and autumn, they rasp away holes in foliage, leaving trails of silver slime behind them. There are a number of controls, both chemical and organic: for the ultimate in natural methods, prowl the garden on damp evenings by flashlight, picking off the pests by hand and disposing of them where they can do no harm.

Chemical controls Slug pellets and dusts containing chemical ingredients such as methiocarb control both slugs and snails. Some are now labeled as safe for children and pets, but, even so, family gardeners may prefer not to use them.

Biological control Parasites such as *Phasmarhabditis hermaphrodita* will destroy slugs and snails. Some garden centers stock them, or they are available through mail order. Most suppliers recommend applying it twice, with a two-week interval.

Traps and barriers A mulch of sharp grit or diatomaceous earth sometimes helps deter these pests. Among the traps that gardeners find effective, a dish of beer sunk into the ground and an upside-down empty grapefruit half are the most popular. The trap's contents can be disposed of in the morning.

A CALENDAR OF SEASONAL REMINDERS

SPRING
- As soon as soil is workable, plant and mulch new perennials.
- Clump-forming summer- and autumn-flowering perennials that are overcrowded can be lifted, carefully split into portions with shoots and plenty of roots, and replanted, spaced more widely apart.
- Remove dead leaves from plant crowns.
- Plant or transplant evergreen shrubs.
- Prune established evergreen shrubs and shrubs that flower after mid-summer.
- Apply fertilizer to established plants, followed by a mulch onto damp, weed-free soil.
- Where necessary, set in place supports for tall-stemmed perennials.
- Divide crowded bulbs after flowering; make a note of bare spots that could be filled with new bulbs in autumn.

SUMMER
- Divide and replant crowded clumps of spring bulbs before foliage fades.
- Make a note of where summer perennials could be planted to hide the dying foliage of spring bulbs.
- Check that creeping, rooting perennials are not overwhelming others. You can dig up rooted portions and use them to plant up bare ground elsewhere.
- Set out young annuals and bedding plants.
- Check for and deal with pests and diseases as seen.
- Clear weeds and replenish mulches as necessary.
- Keep new plantings well watered until established. Pay special attention to watering plants in containers.
- Prune spring-flowering shrubs after flowering.
- If necessary, deadhead perennials and shrubs after flowering.

AUTUMN
- Plant young biennials in their flowering site.
- Clump-forming spring-flowering perennials that are overcrowded can be lifted, carefully split into portions with shoots and plenty of roots, and replanted more widely apart.
- Plant spring-flowering bulbs.
- Clear autumn leaves and make leaf mold.
- Add disease-free, dead plant material to compost pile.
- Apply dry mulches of straw, hay, or conifer branches to plants that need winter protection, especially in areas without snow cover.
- Plant bare-root shrubs or trees during mild weather when the soil is workable. Water them in thoroughly until winter, and mulch well. Withhold fertilizer in the first year after planting to encourage the roots to search more widely for nutrients.

WINTER
- Peruse catalogs from nurseries to select new plants for your garden.
- Where branches are small enough to be handled safely, remove those that are too low from deciduous trees to let in more light. To remove large branches from mature trees, consult a qualified arborist.
- Shake snow from trees and shrubs to avoid breakage.
- Protect vulnerable plants in containers from severe cold and evergreens from cold, dry winds. Garden fleece, burlap, straw, or plastic bubble-wrap can be used.
- Identify suitable gaps for an early-flowering shrub, and make a note of planting sites for late winter bulbs, such as aconites and snowdrops.
- As spring begins, remove winter mulches and other cold protection only when threat of hard frosts is over.

DEADHEADING RHODODENDRONS
Remove dead flowers by pinching them out with your finger and thumb to avoid damage to the new buds that form directly under the old one.

USING LEAVES
Gather up fallen leaves and decaying fruits and let them decompose to make leaf mold – a soil improver that is particularly enjoyed by acid-loving woodland plants.

PLANTS FOR SHADE

T HE SHADE-LOVING plants here have symbols that indicate their preferred conditions, but many are not unduly demanding. Nearly all are relatively easy to grow and should succeed within the given USDA hardiness zone ranges. More growing tips are given in *Caring for Your Plants (see pp.47–53)*.

KEY TO SYMBOLS ◩ *Prefers partial shade* ◪ *Prefers light or dappled shade* ▣ *Tolerates deep shade* ◊ *Prefers well-drained soil* ◊ *Prefers moist soil* ◊ *Prefers wet soil* ♺ *Needs acidic soil* **Tall** *More than 4ft/1.2m high* **Medium** *2–4ft/60cm–1.2m high* **Small** *Less than 2ft/60cm high Hardiness zone ranges are given as* **Zx–x.**

A

Aconitum (Monkshood)
Medium to tall, herbaceous perennials with lobed leaves and spikes of hooded, blue flowers in mid- to late summer. For informal and mixed or herbaceous borders. All parts are toxic.
◩ ◪ ◊ Z3–8
A. '**Ivorine**' *p.34.* Also recommended: *A. carmichaelii* 'Arendsii', *A. hemsleyanum*, *A. napellus.*

Actaea (Baneberry)
Small to medium clump-forming perennials bearing clusters of white flowers during spring and early summer, followed by red or white berries in autumn. For informal plantings or woodland gardens.
◩ ◪ ▣ ◊ Z4–8
A. alba p.34; A. rubra p.36.

Adiantum venustum
(Himalayan maidenhair fern)
Small, evergreen, spreading fern valued for its black stalks and distinctive, mid-green triangular fronds. New fronds are bright bronze-pink when they emerge in late winter and early spring.
◩ ◪ ◊ Z5–8
A. venustum p.44.

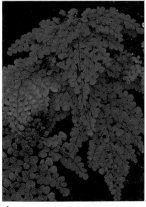
ADIANTUM VENUSTUM

Aesculus parviflora
(Bottlebrush buckeye)
Tall, wide-spreading shrub bearing white flowers in midsummer. Noted for its tolerance of a range of soils and sites. For woodland gardens or shrub borders.
◩ ◪ ◊ ◊ Z5–9

Ajuga (Bugle)
Small, spreading perennials valued for their spikes of deep blue flowers and mats of glossy, often colorful, foliage. For woodland and borders.
◩ ◪ ▣ ◊ ◊ Z3–9
A. pyramidalis p.40;
A. reptans '**Variegata**' *p.26.*

Akebia quinata
(Chocolate vine)
Tall, twining climber bearing purple-brown flowers in spring, followed by purple fruits. For walls, arbors, or through trees.
◩ ◪ ◊ Z5–9

◀SHADY CORNER *Tall, distinctive ferns and variegated foliage create an atmospheric setting.*

Alchemilla (Lady's mantle)
Small, ground-covering,
herbaceous perennials with
silky-haired leaves and sprays
of yellow-green flowers borne
in summer. Self-sows freely.
🔲 🔲 ▣ ◊ ◊ Z3–8
A. mollis p.26. Also
recommended: *A. alpina*,
A. conjuncta.

Amelanchier lamarckii
(Juneberry)
Tall, suckering shrub bearing
sprays of white flowers in
spring and early summer,
followed by purple-black
fruits. Noted for its bronze
foliage in autumn. For
shrub borders or woodland.
🔲 🔲 ◊ ◊ 🌱 Z5–9

Anemone (Windflower)
Tall, autumn-flowering
herbaceous or small, spring-
flowering tuberous perennials
bearing cup-shaped flowers
in white, blue, pink or red.
Thrive in borders and
woodland gardens beneath
deciduous shrubs or trees.
🔲 🔲 ◊ ◊ Z3–9
A. x hybrida 'Honorine
Jobert' p.30; *A. sylvestris*
p.34.

Angelica
Tall, herbaceous plants with
sprays of small, greenish
flowers, followed by ribbed,
brown fruits. Use as focal
points in borders. May self-
sow. Need deep, fertile soil.
🔲 🔲 ▣ ◊ Z4–9
A. archangelica p.26.

Aquilegia vulgaris
(Columbine)
Medium-height herbaceous
perennial valued for its
rosettes of leaves and sprays
of spurred, bell-shaped
flowers in shades of white,
pink, purple, or blue, borne in
late spring and early summer.
For cottage gardens and
herbaceous or mixed borders.
🔲 🔲 ◊ Z3–8
Recommended: 'Norah
Barlow'.

Arctostaphylos uva-ursi
(Bearberry)
Small, evergreen, ground-
covering shrub with tangled
branches bearing small, oval
leaves. Tiny, pink-rimmed
flowers are borne in summer,
followed by red autumn
fruits. For woodland gardens.
🔲 🔲 ◊ 🌱 Z2–6

Arum (Lords-and-ladies)
Small, low-growing perennials
with spear-shaped leaves
marked silvery white, and
hooded spikes of toxic scarlet
berries in early summer.
🔲 🔲 ▣ Z6–10
A. italicum 'Marmoratum'
p.40.

Aruncus dioicus
(Goatsbeard)
Tall perennial grown for its
divided, fernlike leaves and
pyramidal sprays of creamy
white flowers borne in
summer. A moisture-loving
plant for damp borders
or woodland plantings.
🔲 🔲 ▣ ◊ Z3–7

Asarum hartwegii
(Wild ginger)
Small, evergreen, ground-
cover perennial with dark
green leaves that are marbled
silver-green. Tiny, urn-shaped
flowers appear in late spring
and early summer. For border
edges and beneath shrubs.
🔲 🔲 ▣ ◊ Z6–8

Asplenium
Medium, evergreen and semi-
evergreen, upright ferns that
form shuttlecocks of bright
green, leathery fronds, often
with wavy or ruffled margins.
🔲 🔲 ▣ ◊ Z3–11
A. scolopendrium Crispum
Group p.44.

Astilbe
Small to medium, clump-
forming perennials with
divided leaves and plumes of
tiny white, red, or pink
flowers, borne in late spring
or summer. For damp borders
and woodland plantings.
🔲 🔲 ◊ Z4–9
A. 'Irrlicht' p.40.

AQUILEGIA VULGARIS 'NIVEA'

ASTILBE 'FANAL'

Astrantia (Masterwort)
Medium, clump-forming
perennials bearing tiny
flowers with papery, pink or
white bracts in summer. For
damp borders or streamsides.
▨ ▨ ◊ ◊ Z4–8
A. major 'Shaggy' *p.40.*

Athyrium
Small, elegant, deciduous
ferns with arching fronds.
A. niponicum 'Pictum' has
silver-gray segments with
maroon stalks and midribs.
For borders and woodland.
▨ ▨ ◊ Z4–9
A. niponicum 'Pictum'
p.44.

Aucuba japonica
Tall, evergreen shrub with
bold, often variegated leaves
and showy fruits. Valued for
its tolerance of poor soils,
deep shade, and pollution.
For hedging or shrub borders.
▨ ▨ ▣ ◊ ◊ Z6–10
Recommended:
'Crotonifolia'.

B

Bergenia (Elephant's ears)
Small, low-growing, evergreen
perennials grown for their
foliage and pink or white
flowers in late winter and
early spring. For border edges
and woodland gardens.
▨ ▨ ◊ Z3–8
Bergenia purpurascens p.34.

Betula (Birch)
Deciduous trees with
an airy branch structure
and beautiful bark. Use as
specimens or in woodland.
▨ ▨ ◊ Z2–9
B. ermanii 'Grayswood
Hill' *p.40.*

CALLICARPA BODINIERI VAR.
GIRALDII 'PROFUSION'

Blechnum
Small to medium, evergreen,
creeping ferns with leathery,
dark green fronds. Suitable
as a groundcover in damp
borders, woodland gardens,
and ferneries.
▨ ▨ ▣ ◊ 🌣 Z5–11
Recommended: *B. chilense,
B. penna-marina, B. spicant.*

Brunnera macrophylla
Small perennial bearing rich
blue, forget-me-not-like
flowers in spring. Bright green
leaves expand after flowering
to create a good groundcover.
Needs shelter from dry winds.
▨ ▨ ◊ Z3–7
B. macrophylla p.40 and
'Dawson's White' *p.26.*
Also recommended: 'Hadspen
Cream'.

Buxus (Boxwood)
Tall to medium, evergreen,
small-leaved shrubs of
rounded habit. Good for
hedging or topiary; dwarf
cultivars can be used as
edging or in containers.
▨ ▨ ◊ Z6–9
B. sempervirens 'Suffruticosa'
p.30.

CAMPANULA LACTIFLORA
'LODDON ANNA'

C

Callicarpa bodinieri
(Beautyberry)
Tall, deciduous shrub with
small, pink summer flowers
and beadlike, violet fruits in
autumn, borne freely if grown
in groups. For shrub borders.
▨ ◊ Z6–8

Camellia
Tall, elegant, evergreen shrubs
or small trees with glossy,
dark green foliage and showy
pink, red, white, or yellow
flowers borne from mid-
winter to early spring.
Suitable as specimen plants
or for borders and woodland.
▨ ▨ ◊ 🌣 Z7–8

Campanula (Bellflower)
Small to tall herbaceous
perennials valued for their
nodding, bell-shaped flowers
in shades of blue or pink,
borne in summer. For lightly
shaded borders or open
woodland gardens.
▨ ▨ ◊ Z3–9
C. persicifolia 'Telham Beauty'
p.34.

CAREX OSHIMENSIS
'EVERGOLD'

Carex (Sedge)
Medium tufts of evergreen
grasslike leaves, several with
golden foliage. Brown flower
spikelets appear in summer.
Suitable for gravel gardens.
Many are good in containers.
▨ ▨ ◊ Z3–9
C. elata 'Aurea' *p.44.*

Celastrus (Bittersweet)
Tall, vigorous, twining
climbers with scalloped or
toothed, mid-green leaves
and small green flowers in
summer. Grown for their
yellow fruits in autumn,
which split open to reveal
colored seeds. For pergolas,
fences, or walls.
▨ ▨ ◊ ◊ Z4–8

Chaenomeles (Flowering
quince, Japonica)
Tall, deciduous, often spiny
shrubs grown for their white,
red, or pink cup-shaped
spring flowers, followed by
edible, purplish green fruits.
Good against shady walls.
▨ ▨ ◊ ◊ Z5–9
Recommended: *C.* x *superba*
'Crimson and Gold'
and 'Pink Lady'.

Chelidonium majus (Greater
celandine)
Medium, clump-forming
perennial valued for its deeply
divided leaves and yellow,
cup-shaped flowers (double in
'Flore Pleno') in summer. For
woodland or wild gardens.
▨ ▨ ▩ ◊ ◊ Z5–8

Chionodoxa forbesii
(Glory of the snow)
Small bulb with spreading,
bright green leaves and blue,
star-shaped flowers in early
spring. For underplanting.
▨ ◊ Z3–9

Choisya ternata (Mexican
orange blossom)
Tall, evergreen shrub grown
for its glossy leaves and
scented white flowers, borne
in spring and summer. For
courtyards and borders.
▨ ▨ ◊ Z8–10

Cimicifuga racemosa
(Bugbane)
Tall, clump-forming perennial
bearing tiny white flowers
in summer. For woodland
gardens or borders.
▨ ▨ ◊ Z3–8

CHAENOMELES SPECIOSA
'MOERLOOSEI'

CLEMATIS 'NELLY MOSER'

Clematis
Tall, evergreen and deciduous
climbers grown for their mass
of showy flowers, which are
often followed by decorative
seedheads. For training into
host plants or on walls.
▨ ▨ ◊ Z4–9
C. 'Alba Luxurians' *p.30;*
C. rehderiana p.30.

Clethra alnifolia
(Sweet pepperbush)
Tall, clump-forming shrub
with spikes of fragrant white
flowers in summer. For
woodland or borders.
▨ ▨ ◊ ◊ Z3–9

Convallaria
(Lily-of-the-valley)
Small herbaceous perennials
with sprays of scented, waxy
white flowers. Suitable as
a groundcover under trees.
Can be invasive.
▨ ▨ ▩ ◊ Z2–7

Cornus mas
Tall, vigorous, deciduous
shrub distinguished by its
yellow blooms borne on
bare branches in late winter.
For woodland gardens.
▨ ▨ ◊ Z5–8

COTONEASTER
'ROTHSCHILDIANUS'

Corydalis lutea
Small perennial grown for its fernlike foliage and spurred yellow flowers from late spring to autumn. For woodland or borders.
■ ■ ◊ ◊ Z5–8

Corylopsis pauciflora
Tall, deciduous shrub bearing drooping, bell-shaped, pale yellow flowers on bare branches in spring. For shrub borders or woodland gardens.
■ ■ ◊ ◊ Z6–9

Corylus maxima (Filbert)
Tall, deciduous shrub grown for its foliage, spring catkins, and edible nuts. For borders or as informal hedging.
■ ■ ▣ ◊ ◊ Z4–9

Cotoneaster
Ranging in height from small to tall, deciduous or evergreen shrubs and trees grown for their foliage, spring flowers, and autumn berries. Good for informal screens, hedges, shrub borders, and woodland gardens.
■ ■ ◊ Z5–9

Cyclamen hederifolium
(Baby cyclamen)
Small perennial with nodding, pink or white flowers in autumn, followed by mats of dark green leaves with silver marbling. Underplant beneath shrubs or conifers. Tolerates dry soils.
■ ■ ◊ Z8–9
Recommended: 'Albiflorum'.

D

Danae racemosa
(Alexandrian laurel)
Medium, clump-forming, evergreen perennial grown for its slender shoots and glossy leaves. Spikes of tiny, yellow-green flowers are borne in early summer, followed by glossy, bright red berries in autumn. For woodland gardens or shrub groupings.
■ ■ ◊ Z6–9

Dicentra
Small to medium perennials valued for their fernlike leaves and sprays of drooping, heart-shaped flowers in white, yellow, pink, or red, produced in spring and summer. For borders or woodland gardens.
■ ■ ◊ ◊ Z3–9
D. spectabilis 'Alba' *p.34.*
Also recommended:
D. 'Bacchanal', *D.* 'Pearl Drops', *D. spectabilis.*

Digitalis purpurea
(Foxglove)
Tall biennial or short-lived perennial noted for its spires of pink, red, purple, or white, bell-shaped flowers, borne in summer. For herbaceous or mixed borders. Good for naturalizing in woodland.
■ ■ ◊ Z4–8

Dryopteris
Medium, deciduous ferns with arching fronds. For wild or woodland gardens and ferneries.
■ ■ ▣ ◊ Z3–10
Recommended:
D. erythrosora.

E

Enkianthus campanulatus
Tall, deciduous shrub valued for its small, cream and red urn-shaped flowers in spring and early summer, followed by colorful autumn leaves. For borders or woodland.
■ ■ ◊ Z5–8

Epimedium grandiflorum
(Barrenwort)
Small, clump-forming perennial grown for its heart-shaped leaves, which are colorful when young and in autumn. Spurred, cup- or saucer-shaped flowers appear in spring and early summer. For woodland or borders.
■ ■ ◊ Z5–8
Recommended: 'Crimson Beauty' and 'Rose Queen'.

ENKIANTHUS
CAMPANULATUS

EUONYMUS FORTUNEI
'SILVER QUEEN'

Eranthis hyemalis
(Winter aconite)
Small perennial grown for its cup-shaped yellow flowers with distinctive, bright green ruffs, borne in late winter or early spring. Use among shrubs and trees or naturalize in thin grass.
▨ ▨ ◊ ◊ Z4–9

Erythronium
(Dog's-tooth violet)
Small, clump-forming bulbous perennials grown for their drooping spring flowers in shades of white, yellow, pink, or purple. For underplanting trees and shrubs.
▨ ▨ ◊ Z3–9
Recommended: *E. californicum* 'White Beauty' , *E. oreganum*, *E. revolutum*.

Euonymus fortunei cultivars
Small to medium shrubs or climbers, valued for their often white- or golden-variegated foliage. For groundcover or borders. May be scrambled up trees.
▨ ▨ ◊ ◊ Z5–9
Recommended:
'Emerald 'n' Gold'.

FOTHERGILLA MAJOR

Euphorbia
Annuals and perennials that vary in size, most with eye-catching yellow-green, or sometimes flame-colored heads of cup-shaped bracts in spring and summer. Tolerate deep shade and dry soils. Will self-sow.
▣ ▨ ▨ ◊ ◊ Z4–9
E. characias subsp. *wulfenii* p.26. Also recommended: *E. amygdaloides* var. *robbiae*.

F

Fargesia
Tall, evergreen, clump-forming bamboos with bright green leaves contrasted against yellow or purple-brown stems. For borders and woodland gardens.
▨ ▨ ◊ Z5–10
Recommended: *F. murieliae*, *F. nitida*.

✕ *Fatshedera lizei*
Tall, evergreen shrub with large sprays of cream flowers borne in autumn. Tie in against shady walls in courtyards and borders.
▨ ▨ ◊ ◊ Z8–10

Fothergilla major
Tall, deciduous upright shrub with fragrant, white bottlebrush flowers in spring and early summer, and brilliant autumn color. Suitable for borders and woodland gardens.
▨ ▨ ◊ ◊ Z5–8

G

Galanthus nivalis
(Snowdrop)
Small, bulbous perennial grown for its drooping white, pear-shaped flowers, borne in late winter and spring. For underplanting beneath shrubs in borders or naturalizing in grass or woodland.
▨ ▨ ▣ ◊ Z3–9
Recommended: 'Flore Pleno'.

Galium odoratum
(Sweet woodruff)
Small, low-growing, spreading perennial with slender leaves and tiny, scented, star-shaped white flowers produced from spring to summer. Ground-cover for woodland gardens or beneath shrubs in borders.
▨ ▨ ◊ ◊ Z5–8

GALIUM ODORATUM

Garrya elliptica
Tall, evergreen shrub or small tree bearing long, silver-gray catkins from midwinter to spring. For shady walls and borders.
🔲 🗹 ◊ ◊ Z8–10
Recommended: 'James Roof'.

Gaultheria mucronata
Medium, evergreen shrub, with a dense, bushy habit, valued for its glossy dark green foliage, urn-shaped white flowers, and large, showy pink, crimson, or white fruits. For woodland gardens.
🔲 🗹 ◊ 凸 Z8–9
Recommended: 'Mulberry Wine' and 'Wintertime'.

Gentiana asclepiadea
(Willow gentian)
Medium perennial noted for its rich blue trumpet-shaped blooms, borne in summer and autumn. For shady borders and woodland gardens. May naturalize in ideal conditions.
🔲 🗹 ◊ 凸 Z6–9
G. asclepiadea p.36.

Geranium (Cranesbill)
Small to medium perennials valued for their lobed, often aromatic leaves and saucer-shaped flowers in shades of white, pink, purple, or blue. Suitable as groundcover beneath shrubs, in borders, or woodland gardens.
🔲 🗹 ◊ ◊ Z4–9
G. phaeum and '**Album**' *p.30.*

Gymnocarpium dryopteris
Small, deciduous, ground-covering fern noted for its distinctive triangular fronds. For borders, ferneries, and woodland gardens.
🔲 🗹 ◊ Z4–8

H

Hakonechloa macra
Small, clump-forming perennial grass valued for its reddish autumn tints. For shady borders or woodland.
🔲 🗹 ◊ ◊ Z5–9
H. macra '**Aureola**' *p.36.*

Halesia carolina (Silverbell)
Deciduous tree with white, bell-shaped flowers during spring or early summer, and colorful autumn foliage. For woodland or shrub borders.
🔲 🗹 ◊ ◊ Z5–8

Hamamelis (Witch hazel)
Tall, deciduous shrubs valued for their autumn color and scented, yellow, spidery flowers in winter or early spring.
🔲 🗹 ◊ ◊ Z3–9

Hedera (Ivy)
Evergreen climbers, often with variegated leaves. For walls or as a groundcover. Tolerate dry shade.
🔲 🗹 ◊ Z5–10
H. helix 'Buttercup' *p.26;*
H. helix 'Glacier' *p.40.*

HEDERA HELIX '*PEDATA*'

HEPATICA NOBILIS '*JAPONICA*'

Helleborus (Hellebore)
Small, clump-forming, sometimes evergreen perennials with lobed or divided leaves and saucer-shaped flowers in white and shades of cream, pink, green, or purple, borne from late winter to spring. For shrub or mixed borders. May be naturalized in woodland.
🔲 🗹 ◊ Z4–9
H. niger 'Potter's Wheel' *p.40;*
H. x hybridus 'Ballard's Black' *p.40.*

Hepatica nobilis
Small, semi-evergreen, clump-forming perennial with bowl-shaped white, pink or blue flowers borne in early spring. For border edges and woodland gardens.
🔲 🗹 ◊ Z5–8

Heuchera (Coral bells)
Small, fully or semi-evergreen perennials bearing spikes of tiny pink, red, or greenish flowers in spring and summer. Use as a groundcover in borders or woodland gardens.
🔲 🗹 ▣ ◊ ◊ Z3–8
H. 'Pewter Moon' *p.40.* Also recommended: *H. cylindrica*.

HYDRANGEA SERRATA
'BLUEBIRD'

Hosta
Small to medium perennials valued for their foliage, with flowers borne above the leaves in mid- to late summer. Good groundcover.
🔳 🔲 🔳 ◊ Z3–8
'Albomarginata' *p.44*;
'Birchwood Parky's Gold'
p.26; 'Frances Williams'
p.30; 'Gold Standard' *p.26*.

Hyacinthoides hispanica
(Spanish bluebell)
Small, bulbous perennial bearing nodding, bell-shaped, blue flowers in spring. For underplanting in woodland gardens or shrub borders.
🔳 🔲 ◊ Z4–9

Hydrangea
Medium to tall shrubs and one self-clinging climber, *H. anomala*, grown for their lacecap or mophead flower-heads in white and shades of pink or blue, in late summer. For borders or woodland.
🔳 🔲 ◊ Z4–9
H. paniculata 'Grandiflora'
p.36; *H. anomala* subsp.
petiolaris p.40;
H. quercifolia p.30.

Hypericum (St. John's wort)
Medium evergreen, semi-evergreen, and deciduous shrubs valued for their showy yellow flowers. Those recommended tolerate poor, dry soils and make good groundcovers.
🔳 🔲 ◊ ◊ Z4–10
Recommended: *H. andro-saemum, H. calycinum.*

I

Ilex (Holly)
Tall, mostly evergreen shrubs and trees with colorful winter-persistent fruits and attractive foliage. Cultivars variegated with cream, white, or gold need more light than green-leaved forms. May be clipped.
🔳 🔲 ◊ ◊ Z5–9
Recommended: *I. glabra,*
I. × meserveae, I. opaca.

Impatiens
Small bedding plants that produce small, flat, brightly colored flowers throughout summer. For borders and containers.
🔳 🔲 ◊ Min. 40°F

HYPERICUM ANDROSAEMUM
'ALBURY PURPLE'

Iris sibirica (Siberian iris)
Medium-height, beardless iris with narrow, grasslike leaves and dark-veined, white, red-violet, blue, or blue-purple flowers, borne in late spring and early summer. For watersides and borders.
🔳 ◊ Z4–9
'Caesar's Brother' *p.34*.

Itea virginica (Sweetspire, Tassel-white)
Tall, deciduous shrub with colorful autumn foliage and upright spikes of fragrant, creamy white flowers, borne in summer. For shrub borders or open glades in woodland.
🔳 🔲 ◊ ◊ Z6–9

J

Jasminum nudiflorum
(Winter jasmine)
Tall, slender, deciduous shrub valued for its bright yellow flowers produced on bare stems in winter and early spring. Needs support when grown as a climber. For pergolas, arbors, or walls.
🔳 🔲 ◊ ◊ Z6–9

ILEX AQUIFOLIUM
'ARGENTEA MARGINATA'

Jeffersonia (Twinleaf)
Small perennial grown for
its lobed leaves and cup-
shaped, white or lavender
flowers, borne on long,
slender stalks in late spring
and early summer. Suitable
for damp sites.
🔲 🔲 ▣ ◊ Z5–8

K

Kirengeshoma palmata
Medium to tall perennial
with maplelike leaves and
waxy, pale yellow flowers in
late summer and autumn. For
woodland gardens or borders.
🔲 🔲 ◊ ♉ Z5–8

L

Lamium (Deadnettle)
Small, spreading perennials
with wrinkled, often marked
leaves and small pink or
white flowers from early
spring to summer. Good
groundcovers.
🔲 🔲 ▣ ◊ ◊ Z4–8
L. maculatum 'Beacon Silver'
p.40.

*KIRENGESHOMA
PALMATA*

LAMIUM MACULATUM 'ALBUM'

Leucojum vernum
(Spring snowflake)
Small, bulbous perennial
valued for its nodding, bell-
shaped white flowers in early
and late spring. For woodland
gardens and borders.
🔲 🔲 ◊ Z4–8

Leucothöe fontanesiana
Tall, evergreen shrub with
arching, zig-zag branches,
glossy, dark green foliage, and
sprays of small, urn-shaped
waxy white flowers, borne
in spring. For woodland.
🔲 🔲 ▣ ◊ ♉ Z5–8

Leycesteria formosa
Tall, thicket-forming,
deciduous shrub with unusual
spikes of white flowers with
purple bracts in summer and
early autumn. For borders or
woodland gardens.
🔲 🔲 ◊ Z9–10

Lilium (Lily)
Tall, elegant bulbous
perennials with turkscap
or trumpet-shaped flowers
in summer. For containers
in patios or courtyards.
🔲 🔲 ◊ Z3–8
L. martagon p.36.

Linnaea borealis
(Twinflower)
Small, prostrate, evergreen
shrub noted for its mats of
glossy foliage and bell-shaped,
pale pink flowers in summer.
For woodland gardens.
🔲 🔲 ▣ ◊ ♉ Z2–6

Liriope muscari (Lilyturf)
Evergreen perennial with
narrow leaves and spikes
of violet-mauve flowers in
autumn. Good groundcover.
🔲 🔲 ▣ ◊ ◊ ♉ Z6–10

Lonicera (Honeysuckle)
Tall, evergreen or deciduous,
twining climbers valued for
their often scented summer
flowers in shades of yellow,
white, or red. For arbors,
walls, or through trees.
🔲 🔲 ◊ ◊ Z3–9

Lunaria (Honesty)
Medium-height biennials
and perennials with scented
white, violet, or purple
flowers in summer followed
by flat, silvery seedheads.
For woodland gardens.
🔲 🔲 ◊ ◊ Z5–9
L. annua 'Variegata' *p.26.*

*LEYCESTERIA
FORMOSA*

LUZULA NIVEA

Luzula (Woodrush)
Small to medium evergreen rushes forming clumps of flat leaves. The small flowers are ornamentally insignificant in most. Use as low groundcover in damp sites.
▣ ▨ ◊ Z4–11
Recommended: *L. sylvatica* 'Aurea' and 'Marginata'.

M

Mahonia aquifolium
(Oregon grapeholly)
Small, evergreen shrub valued for its scented yellow or orange flowers in spring. For tall groundcover in borders or woodland gardens.
▣ ▨ ▩ ◊ ◊ Z6–9
Recommended: 'Orange Flame' and 'Smaragd'.

Maianthemum bifolium
(May lily)
Small, ground-covering perennial grown for its glossy leaves and spikes of tiny, star-shaped white flowers, borne in spring. Suitable for wild gardens or woodland plantings.
▣ ▨ ▩ ◊ ᵔ Z4–7

Matteuccia (Ostrich fern)
Tall, deciduous fern with arching, pale green fronds, followed by dark brown fertile fronds that form in the center of the shuttlecock in late summer. For woodland gardens, shady borders, ferneries, and at poolsides. Can be invasive.
▣ ▨ ◊ Z3–8
M. struthiopteris p.44.

Meconopsis cambrica
(Welsh poppy)
Small perennial with deeply cut, blue-green leaves and poppylike, yellow or orange flowers produced from spring to autumn. Suitable for woodland plantings, wild gardens, and informal borders. Self-seeds freely.
▣ ▨ ◊ Z6–8
M. cambrica pp.26 and 44.

Myosotis sylvatica
(Forget-me-not)
Small biennial with yellow-eyed blue, pink, or white flowers in spring and early summer. For woodland or wild gardens, or beneath shrubs in borders.
▣ ▨ ◊ ◊ Z5–9

MATTEUCCIA STRUTHIOPTERIS

N

Nicotiana (Flowering tobacco)
Medium-height annuals and perennials with scented and subtly colored trumpet-shaped flowers, borne for long periods in summer. For beds, borders, or containers.
▣ ▨ ◊ ◊ Z10–11
N. sylvestris p.36;
N. 'Lime Green' p.30.

O

Omphalodes (Navelwort)
Small, evergreen perennials bearing forget-me-not-like blue flowers in early spring. Suitable as a groundcover in woodland gardens.
▣ ▨ ◊ Z6–9

Ornithogalum
(Star-of-Bethlehem)
Small bulbs grown for their starry white flowers borne in spring or early summer. For shrub or mixed borders. May be naturalized in grass.
▣ ▨ ◊ Z5–10
Recommended: *O. nutans.*

Osmanthus x burkwoodii
Tall, dense, evergreen shrub bearing small clusters of tiny white, scented flowers in mid- to late spring, followed by blue-black berries. For large pots, borders, or hedging.
▣ ▨ ◊ Z7–9

Osmunda
Medium, deciduous ferns with triangular fronds that turn golden brown in autumn. For ferneries and watersides.
▣ ▨ ◊ ᵔ Z4–9
O. cinnamomea p.44.

P

Pachyphragma macrophyllum
Small, mat-forming, semi-evergreen perennial valued for its clusters of tiny white flowers, borne during early spring. For groundcover beneath trees and shrubs.
◩ ◪ ◊ Z5–9

Pachysandra
Small, fully or semi-evergreen, spreading perennials bearing coarsely toothed, dark green leaves and spikes of tiny white flowers in summer. Tolerates poor, dry soils. Excellent groundcovers.
◩ ◪ ✳ ◊ ◊ Z4–9
P. terminalis p.40. Also recommended: 'Variegata'.

Parthenocissus henryana
(Chinese Virginia creeper) Tall, deciduous climber noted for its dark green, white-veined foliage, often pink-centered, and brilliant autumn color. For training on walls or fences, or through trees.
◩ ◪ ◊ ◊ Z6–8

Phegopteris (Beech fern)
Small, attractive, carpet-forming ferns with soft, pale green fronds. For woodland gardens, ferneries, or damp, sheltered borders.
◩ ◪ ✳ ◊ 凹 Z3–8
P. connectilis pp.36 and 44.

Photinia
Tall, deciduous or evergreen shrubs and trees grown for their foliage and clusters of small white flowers, borne in spring. For borders, informal hedging, or woodland.
◩ ◪ ◊ Z4–9

PHOTINIA x FRASERI 'RED ROBIN'

Pieris japonica
Medium evergreen shrub with leathery, dark green leaves (bronze when young) and clusters of waxy white flowers in late winter or spring. For shrub borders, woodland, or large containers.
◩ ◪ ◊ 凹 Z6–8

Podophyllum
Small perennials with white or pink, cup-shaped flowers in spring and early summer. For woodland or damp borders. All parts are toxic.
◩ ◪ ✳ ◊ Z4–9

PODOPHYLLUM HEXANDRUM

POLEMONIUM PAUCIFLORUM 'PURPUREUS'

Polemonium (Jacob's ladder)
Small, clump-forming perennials with usually white or blue, bell-shaped flowers borne in spring and summer. For borders or wild garden. Some may be naturalized in grass. Self-seeds freely.
◩ ◪ ◊ ◊ Z4–9
Recommended: *P. caeruleum*, *P.* 'Lambrook Mauve'.

Polygonatum
(Solomon's seal) Medium to tall, elegant perennials with bell-shaped, green-white flowers that hang from arching stems in spring or summer. For borders or woodland gardens.
◩ ◪ ✳ ◊ Z3–9
P. x *hybridum* p.34. Also recommended: *P. biflorum*.

Polypodium
Small, robust, evergreen ferns with arching, leathery fronds, some of which are crested or curled. Use as a groundcover in ferneries, shady borders, or woodland.
◩ ◪ ◊ Z4–11
P. vulgare 'Cornubiense' p.44.

PYRACANTHA
'ORANGE GLOW'

Polystichum

Small to medium, evergreen ferns valued for their shuttlecocks of finely divided, fresh green fronds. Suitable for borders and ferneries or woodland gardens.
▣ ▣ ▣ ◊ Z3–9
P. setiferum Divisilobum Group *pp.34* and *44*.

Primula florindae

(Giant cowslip)
Medium, deciduous perennial grown for its toothed, mid-green leaves and slender, funnel-shaped, scented yellow flowers. Suitable for informal plantings, containers, damp borders, and woodland plantings.
▣ ▣ ◊ Z3–8
P. florindae p.34.

Prunus laurocerasus

(Cherry laurel)
Tall, compact, evergreen shrub valued for its spikes of white flowers borne in spring, with cherrylike black fruits in autumn. Tolerates pollution and most soil conditions.
▣ ▣ ▣ ◊ ◊ Z6–9
Recommended: 'Zabeliana'.

Pulmonaria (Lungwort)

Small perennials with funnel-shaped flowers in white, blue, pink, or purple, borne in late winter or early spring. For borders or woodland.
▣ ▣ ▣ ◊ Z4–8
P. 'Mawson's Blue' *p.40;*
P. officinalis 'Sissinghurst White' *p.40.*

Pyracantha (Firethorn)

Tall, spiny evergreen shrubs with white summer flowers and winter berries. For walls, mixed borders, and hedging.
▣ ▣ ◊ Z5–9

R

Ranunculus

Small to medium perennials with white or yellow, saucer-shaped flowers in spring and early summer. For damp borders or woodland.
▣ ▣ ▣ ◊ Z4–9

Rheum palmatum

Tall perennial with rhubarb-like leaves and spires of cream or dark red flowers in summer. For damp borders.
▣ ▣ ◊ Z5–9

RIBES ODORATUM

Rhododendron

Evergreen and deciduous shrubs and trees that range widely in height, grown for their impressive, sometimes scented spring flowers. For many uses.
▣ ▣ ◊ ⌘ Z3–9

Rhodotypos scandens

Tall, deciduous shrub with papery white flowers in late spring, followed by shiny black berries. For woodland or shrub borders.
▣ ▣ ◊ ◊ Z5–8

Ribes odoratum

Medium, compact, deciduous shrubs grown for their clusters of bell-shaped, pink, white or greenish yellow flowers borne in spring. For informal hedging and borders.
▣ ◊ ◊ Z2–6

Rodgersia pinnata

Tall, clump-forming perennial with crinkled lobed leaves, reddish green stems, and spires of white, pink, or red flowers borne in late summer. For damp borders, watersides, and at woodland margins.
▣ ▣ ◊ Z5–8

RODGERSIA PINNATA 'SUPERBA'

Rosa 'New Dawn'

Rosa (Roses)
The Alba group of old garden roses is tall and tolerant of shade. Many ramblers and climbers tolerate some shade on their lower halves, given good light on their top growth. For pergolas, arbors, and walls.
🏵 🌣 ◊ Z3–9
R. 'Albéric Barbier' *p.30;*
R. 'New Dawn' *p.30.*

Rubus tricolor
Medium, prostrate, evergreen shrub with glossy foliage, red-bristled shoots, and cup-shaped white flowers borne in summer, followed by edible red fruits in autumn. Use as a groundcover in shrub borders.
🏵 🌣 🌣 ◊ Z7–9

Ruscus (Broom)
Small to medium, shrubby evergreens with flattened, leaflike shoots that bear tiny white, star-shaped flowers and glossy red fruits from late summer to winter. For dry borders.
🏵 🌣 🌣 ◊ Z4–10
R. aculeatus *p.26.*
Also recommended:
R. hypoglossum.

S

Sambucus nigra
(Black elder)
Tall, deciduous shrub grown for its sprays of small, white to ivory flowers, followed by black, white, or red fruits. Tolerates poor, dry, or wet soils and pollution.
🏵 🌣 ◊ ◊ Z6–8
Recommended: 'Aurea', 'Guincho Purple' and 'Laciniata'.

Sanguinaria canadensis
(Bloodroot)
Small perennial with heart-shaped, blue-green, scalloped leaves and white flowers in spring. For woodland and borders.
🏵 🌣 🌣 ◊ Z3–9
Recommended: 'Plena'.

Sarcococca (Christmas box)
Medium, ground-covering, evergreen shrubs bearing fragrant, white or whitish green flowers in winter. For shrub borders and dry soils.
🏵 🌣 🌣 ◊ Z6–10
Recommended: S. hookeriana, S. humilis, S. ruscifolia.

Saxifraga granulata

Saxifraga (Saxifrage)
Small, clump-forming, evergreen perennial with rosettes of leaves and small, white or pink, star- or cup-shaped flowers in spring. Suitable as a groundcover, even in poor soil. For borders and woodland gardens.
🏵 🌣 ◊ ◊ Z6–7
Recommended: S. granulata 'Plena', S. x urbium (London pride).

Schizophragma integrifolium
Tall, elegant, deciduous climber with long-stalked, dark green leaves and large, showy, lacecap flowerheads in summer. Suitable for training on walls, fences, pergolas, and arbors, or through large trees.
🏵 🌣 ◊ ◊ Z5–9

Scilla siberica
(Siberian squill)
Small, bulbous perennials bearing nodding, bowl-shaped, bright blue flowers in spring. Good for underplanting among shrubs and trees. May be naturalized in woodland gardens.
🏵 🌣 ◊ ◊ Z5–8

Shortia
Evergreen, ground-covering perennials valued for their rounded, dark green leaves that turn red in autumn, and funnel-shaped, white or deep pink flowers with deeply fringed petals, borne during spring. Suitable for damp borders or woodland plantings.
🏵 🌣 🌣 ◊ Z5–9
Recommended: S. galacifolia, S. soldanelloides, S. uniflora 'Grandiflora'.

SKIMMIA JAPONICA
'BRONZE KNIGHT'

Skimmia japonica
Medium to tall, evergreen, spring-flowering shrub valued for its slightly aromatic leaves and fragrant white flowers, which open from red buds. Tolerates pollution. For containers, borders, or woodland gardens.
Z7–9
Recommended: 'Rubella'.

Smilacina racemosa
(False Solomon's seal)
Medium, clump-forming perennial with unbranched, often arching stems, bright green foliage, and dense plumes of tiny cream flowers, borne in spring. For damp borders and woodland.
Z4–9

Sorbaria
Tall, deciduous shrubs valued for their finely divided leaves and sprays of white, starlike flowers produced from mid- to late summer. For shrub borders and woodland or wild gardens.
Z2–10
S. tomentosa var. *angustifolia* p.40.

Stylophorum diphyllum
Small perennial grown for its deeply cut leaves and poppy-like yellow flowers borne in spring. For damp borders, or may be naturalized in woodland. May self-sow.
Z6–9

Styrax
Elegant, deciduous trees noted for their fragrant, bell-shaped white flowers, borne in summer. Some have good autumn color. For sheltered woodland gardens.
Z6–9
S. japonicus p.34. Also recommended: *S. obassia.*

Symphoricarpos
(Snowberry)
Tall, deciduous, thicket-forming shrubs grown mainly for their tiny, bell-shaped flowers, which are highly attractive to bees, and their white, pink, or dark blue, winter-persistent fruits. Tolerate pollution, poor soil, and exposure. For hedging or screens.
Z3–7

STYLOPHORUM DIPHYLLUM

TELLIMA GRANDIFLORA

T

Taxus (Yew)
Tall, evergreen, coniferous shrubs or trees valued for their peeling, red-brown bark and dark green, needlelike leaves and red, winter-persistent fruits. Use as specimens or for hedging.
Z4–8
Recommended: x *media* 'Hicksii'.

Tellima grandiflora
(Fringe cup)
Small, rosette-forming perennial with slender spikes of green-white flowers in spring and summer. Drought-tolerant groundcover for borders or woodland gardens.
Z4–8

Tiarella cordifolia
(Foam flower)
Small, vigorous, groundcover perennial with heart-shaped leaves tinted bronze-red in autumn, and upright spikes of tiny cream flowers in summer. For borders or woodland gardens.
Z3–7

Tolmiea menziesii
(Piggyback plant)
Small, dense, fast-spreading
perennial grown for its pale
green or yellow-green foliage
and small, greenish purple
flowers borne in late spring
and early summer. The leaves
of 'Taff's Gold' are spotted
and mottled cream and pale
yellow. Use as a groundcover
beneath shrubs or trees.
▨ ▨ ✳ ◊ ◑ Z6–9
Recommended: 'Taff's
Gold'.

Trachystemon orientale
Small to medium perennial
with heart-shaped leaves
and blue flowers borne
during spring. Use as a
groundcover in wild and
woodland gardens.
▨ ▨ ◊ ◑ Z6–8

Tricyrtis (Toad lily)
Medium perennials with
prominently veined, pale
to dark green leaves and star-
or funnel-shaped, yellow-
or maroon-speckled flowers
produced from late summer
into autumn. For woodland
gardens or borders.
▨ ▨ ✳ ◊ Z4–9
T. hirta p.36. Also
recommended: *T. formosana.*

Trillium
Small perennials noted
for their net-veined leaves,
often with silver or purple
marbling, and nodding or
upright cup-shaped flowers
in shades of white, pink,
maroon, or yellow, borne in
spring. For borders
or woodland plantings.
▨ ▨ ◊ Z4–9
Recommended:
T. grandiflorum, T. ovatum,
T. rivale, T. sessile.

U

Uvularia grandiflora
(Large merrybells)
Small, elegant perennial with
nodding, yellow, bell-shaped
flowers in spring. For damp
borders or woodland gardens.
▨ ▨ ✳ ◊ Z3–7

V

Vancouveria
Small groundcover perennial
bearing airy sprays of spurred
white flowers in late spring.
For woodland gardens.
▨ ▨ ◊ Z5–8
V. hexandra p.36.

Viburnum
Tall, deciduous and evergreen
shrubs valued for their showy,
often fragrant flowers and
glossy fruits. Use as specimens
in shrub borders, woodland
gardens, or large containers.
▨ ▨ ◊ ◊ Z4–9
Recommended:
V. acerifolium,
V. x burkwoodii, V. nudum,
V. plicatum f. *tomentosum.*

Viola riviniana Purpurea
Group

Vinca minor (Periwinkle)
Small, evergreen, ground-
covering shrub with dark
green leaves and white, blue,
blue-violet, or pink flowers
from spring to autumn. For
woodland gardens, shady
banks, and shrub borders.
▨ ▨ ✳ ◊ ◊ Z4–9

Viola odorata
Small ground-covering
perennial with toothed, heart-
shaped leaves and sweetly
scented, white or blue-violet
flowers from late winter to
spring. For wild gardens or
woodland. Will self-sow.
▨ ▨ ◊ Z8–9
Also recommended:
V. riviniana.

W

Waldsteinia ternata
Small, spreading, semi-
evergreen perennial with
saucer-shaped, bright yellow
flowers borne in late spring
and early summer. Use as
a groundcover beneath trees
or at the front of borders.
▨ ▨ ✳ ◊ Z3–8

Waldsteinia
ternata

INDEX

ACKNOWLEDGMENTS

Picture research Neale Chamberlain, Catherine Costelloe, Sam Ruston

Illustrations Gill Tomblin, Karen Cochrane

Index Hilary Bird

Jacket DK jackets department

DK Publishing would like to thank:
Susanne Mitchell and Barbara Haynes, RHS.

American Horticultural Society
Visit AHS at www.ahs.org or call them at 1-800-777-7931 ext. 10. Membership benefits include *The American Gardener* magazine, free admission to flower shows, the free seed exchange, book services, and the Gardener's Information Service.

Photography
The publisher would like to thank the following for their kind permission to reproduce the photographs:
(key: l=left, r=right, b=bottom, t=top)

A-Z Botanical Collection: A Young 15tr, Christopher Knight 23tl, J Malcolm Smith 9tl
Garden Picture Library: Henk Dijkman 21tl, 24, John Miller 6, Roger Hyam 38, Steven Wooster 28
John Glover: 7bl, 15tl
Jerry Harpur: 12b, Philip Watson 11br
Andrew Lawson: 8b, 25bl, 29bl, Brook Cottage Alkerton 43bl, Designer: Wendy Lauderdale 32
Clive Nichols: White Windows, Hampshire 39bl
Photos Horticultural: 10br, 18b, 42
Harry Smith Collection: 9tr, 11tl, 13br
Elizabeth Whiting & Associates: 54

Jacket photography:
Garden Picture Library: Steven Wooster back tr; **Andrew Lawson:** back tc; **S&O Mathews Photography:** back tl, front bl; **Photos Horticultural:** front r